# the ultimate
# HIGH
# FIBRE
## handbook

**BOOST HEALTH • SUPPORT IMMUNITY • LIVE LONGER**

# the ultimate
# HIGH
# FIBRE
## handbook

## JENNY TSCHIESCHE

**hamlyn**

# COOKERY NOTES

Standard level spoon measurements are used in all recipes.

1 tablespoon – one 15ml spoon

1 teaspoon – one 5ml spoon

Both imperial and metric measurements have been given in all recipes. Use one set of measurements only and not a mixture of both.

Milk should be full fat unless otherwise stated.

Fresh herbs should be used unless otherwise stated. If unavailable use dried herbs as an alternative but halve the quantities stated.

Pepper should be freshly ground black pepper unless otherwise stated.

This book includes dishes made with nuts and nut derivatives.

Vegetarians should look for the 'V' symbol on a cheese to ensure it is made with vegetarian rennet.

# CONTENTS

# INTRODUCTION

**Modern diets are overflowing with calories, protein and fat, yet we're starving our bodies of one nutrient that quietly protects our health: fibre. You can follow every rule of healthy eating, but if fibre is missing, you're still vulnerable to a hidden crisis. It's a silent epidemic; everywhere, fibre is overlooked and underestimated. Though we're eating more food than ever before, most people still fall far short of the recommended daily fibre intake. Indeed, fibre has become so scarce in today's diets that the vast majority of us are missing out, leaving our bodies exposed to the unseen dangers of modern malnutrition as never before.**

These days, we are all obsessed with protein and good fats, while carbs... well, they're a permanent part of the wellness conversation. Fat and sugar content emblazon the front of every snack packet – they are a selling point – and fibre is rarely mentioned (though when it is, we tend to overestimate how much we are getting). But fibre is essential. It underpins the health of our gut, metabolism, even our mood.

This fibre deficit is a fact reflected in the rising rates of digestive issues, metabolic diseases and other health concerns. The data clearly shows that people who skimp on fibre are at a much higher risk for serious conditions such as heart disease, type 2 diabetes and colorectal cancer. If you're aiming to support your long-term health, it's worth taking a closer look at fibre and finding simple ways to include more of it in your everyday meals. Even small changes – adding an extra serving of vegetables, choosing wholegrains or tossing some beans into a salad – can make a meaningful difference over time.

In this book, we'll dive deep into the world of fibre: what it is, why it's important and how you can access its benefits with simple but smart food choices.

## WHAT IS FIBRE?

Fibre is the part of plant foods that the body cannot digest or absorb. Unlike sugars, fats and proteins, it moves through the digestive system mostly unchanged, yet it plays an important role in supporting gut health and overall wellbeing. Fibre comes from plant cell walls – the strong structures that give plants their shape – such as the strings in celery, the skins of apples, the outer layers of wholegrains and the seed coats of beans and lentils. Our bodies can't break them down, so instead we partially ferment them in the gut.

It wasn't until the 1970s that researchers started to realize fibre might be missing from our diets, when a low fibre intake began to be linked to chronic disease. The timing is no coincidence: before industrial food systems took over, fibre wasn't really on anyone's radar.

## HOW MUCH FIBRE DO YOU NEED?

Most adults should aim for 25–35g (1–1¼oz) of fibre per day, but the average person in the UK consumes barely 18g (¾oz). However, variety is key, as different types of fibre offer unique benefits, so include a mix of fruits, vegetables, wholegrains, legumes and prebiotic-rich foods in your diet. And that brings us to our next section.

# THE FIBRE FAMILY

When we talk about fibre, we're really referring to a whole family of plant-based carbohydrates. And today, with so many highly processed foods on our shelves – most of them stripped of their natural fibre during processing – knowing what kinds of fibre exist, why they matter and where to find them has become crucial for anyone looking to improve their health.

As a nutritionist, I often see confusion about the different types of fibre – soluble fibre, insoluble fibre, resistant starch and prebiotics – and their specific benefits. Those are all terms you may well have heard, but you might not yet know their role and importance. It's important to understand that each type of fibre offers different health benefits, whether that's supporting heart health, regulating blood sugar, improving digestive regularity or nurturing your gut microbiome. By choosing the right mix of fibre types, you can target specific health objectives more effectively.

Think of the fibre family as a team. Each member plays a unique role in supporting your heart, gut, immune system and more and no single source of fibre can meet all the body's needs. By eating a wide range of plant-based foods, you'll naturally receive a balance of different members of the fibre family, maximizing the health benefits.

Our goal isn't simply to increase fibre intake, but to increase fibre *diversity* – to include as many members of the fibre family as we can in our diets – so let's take a closer look at soluble fibre, insoluble fibre, resistant starch and prebiotics.

## SOLUBLE FIBRE: HEART HELPER & BLOOD SUGAR BALANCER

### What is it?

Soluble fibre dissolves in water, forming a gel-like substance in your gut. This unique property slows down digestion and nutrient absorption.

### Where do we find it?

Oats, oat bran, barley, beans, lentils, apples, citrus fruits, Brussels sprouts and carrots.

### Health Benefits

- Reduces LDL cholesterol[1]: By binding to cholesterol in the digestive tract, soluble fibre helps remove it from the body, reducing heart disease risk.

- Stabilizes blood sugar[2]: It slows the absorption of sugars, preventing spikes and crashes, which is especially important for people with diabetes or insulin resistance.

- Feeds gut bacteria[3]: Many soluble fibres are fermentable, acting as food for beneficial gut microbes.

## INSOLUBLE FIBRE: DIGESTIVE REGULATOR

### What is it?

Insoluble fibre does not dissolve in water. Instead, it adds bulk to stools and acts as a natural 'scrubbing brush' for your digestive tract.

### Where do we find it?

Wholegrains (brown rice, quinoa, wholewheat, bulgur wheat), nuts, seeds, the skins of fruits and vegetables, leafy greens and root vegetables.

### Health Benefits

- Promotes regularity: By increasing stool bulk and speeding up intestinal transit, insoluble fibre helps prevent constipation and supports regular bowel movements.

- Supports colon health: It may reduce the risk of diverticular disease[4] and some types of colorectal cancer[5].

- Satiety: Adds volume to meals, helping you feel full and potentially aiding weight management.

## RESISTANT STARCH: GUT MICROBIOME BOOSTER

### What is it?

Resistant starch is a type of plant-based carbohydrate that resists digestion in the small intestine. Instead, it travels to the large intestine, where it is fermented by gut bacteria.

### Where do we find it?

Green bananas, legumes, wholegrains and some seeds. Most accessibly, cooking and then cooling carbs such as rice, bread, pasta and potatoes, or legumes such as lentils, chickpeas or beans, increases their resistant starch content.

### Health Benefits

- Feeds beneficial bacteria[6]: Fermentation of resistant starch produces short-chain fatty acids (SCFAs), especially butyrate, which nourishes colon cells and reduces inflammation.

- Improves insulin sensitivity[7]: Regular intake can help regulate blood sugar and may reduce the risk of type 2 diabetes.

- Supports digestive health: Increases stool bulk and promotes regularity.

## PREBIOTICS: THE GUT'S FAVOURITE FUEL

### What is it?

Prebiotics are a subset of fibre (often soluble and fermentable) that specifically feed beneficial gut bacteria, helping them thrive. Many foods that are rich in prebiotics are also considered high FODMAP (Fermentable Oligo-, Di-, Monosaccharides and Polyols). This means they can trigger digestive symptoms in people with irritable bowel syndrome (IBS) or other sensitivities. However, not all prebiotic foods are high FODMAP; for example, bananas and certain wholegrains can provide prebiotic benefits while being lower in FODMAPs. If you're following a low FODMAP diet, it's important to choose prebiotic sources that suit your individual tolerance, so you can still support gut health without discomfort. You can find more detail on this on page 37.

### Where do we find it?

Onions, garlic, leeks, asparagus, Jerusalem artichokes, beans, lentils, chickpeas, bananas and wholegrains.

### Health Benefits

- Enhances gut microbiota: Prebiotics stimulate the growth of 'good' bacteria such as Bifidobacteria and Lactobacilli, supporting a balanced microbiome.

- Improves mood[8]: A healthy gut microbiome is linked to improved mental health outcomes, including mood disturbance, anxiety, depression, stress and sleep.

- Produces SCFAs[9]: As with resistant starch, prebiotics are fermented into SCFAs (see page 13), which have anti-inflammatory and protective effects throughout the body.

## WHICH FIBRE WHEN?

It's plain to see that fibre is more than just a digestive aid. It is a cornerstone of overall health.

Here's how to include different fibre types to help you reach your health objectives:

- For digestion: include insoluble fibre from vegetables, nuts and wholegrains.

- For blood sugar: choose soluble fibre from oats, beans and fruit.

- For cholesterol: include beta-glucan-rich foods such as barley and oats.

- For weight regulation: build meals around legumes, wholegrains and vegetables for volume and satiety.

- For nutrient absorption: add prebiotic fibres such as flaxseed, Jerusalem artichokes and chickpeas.

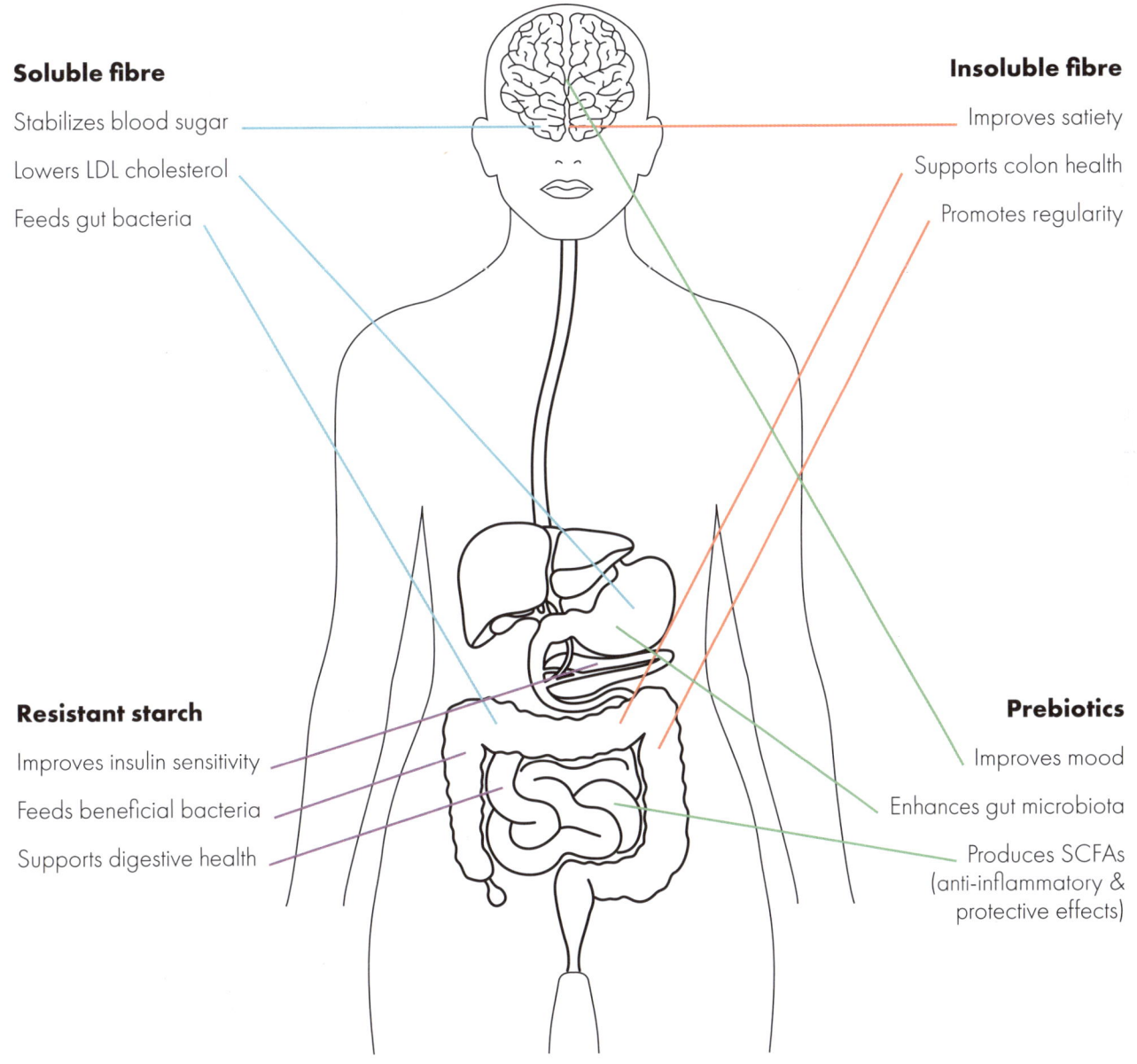

**Soluble fibre**

Stabilizes blood sugar

Lowers LDL cholesterol

Feeds gut bacteria

**Insoluble fibre**

Improves satiety

Supports colon health

Promotes regularity

**Resistant starch**

Improves insulin sensitivity

Feeds beneficial bacteria

Supports digestive health

**Prebiotics**

Improves mood

Enhances gut microbiota

Produces SCFAs
(anti-inflammatory &
protective effects)

# A NOTE ON THE RECIPES

While all these recipes will do you good and are rich in fibre, I have tagged where dishes are particularly useful for specific conditions, or health goals for which fibre can help.

If you're looking to increase the fibre in your diet, you probably have a good reason. Perhaps a health specialist has advised it, or your own research has suggested it. So I've designed seven categories into which the recipes in this book fall, to help you choose which dishes fit your needs the best.

### Low FODMAP

People with IBS (Irritable Bowel Syndrome) often benefit from low FODMAP foods because certain carbohydrates, known as FODMAPs, can trigger uncomfortable digestive symptoms (see page 37 for more details). These recipes have low FODMAPs.

### Heart Heathy

These recipes have soluble fibre, healthy fats and plant sterols for heart protection.

### Weight Loss

High in fibre and protein, these recipes will steady appetite and balance energy.

### Blood Sugar

These recipes are designed to support the liver, hormone clearance and steady blood glucose.

### Mental Clarity

These dishes will be rich in fibre and probiotic foods, to help stabilize your mood.

### Anti-inflammatory

These recipes are rich in polyphenols, omega-3s and fibre synergy.

### For Muscle

For those looking to build muscle, these recipes combine protein, healthy fats and fibre.

# THE FORGOTTEN MACRO: WHY FIBRE DISAPPEARED

For much of human history, fibre was an unremarkable, ever-present part of all our diets. Traditional meals were built around wholegrains, pulses, root vegetables, nuts and seeds and therefore naturally delivered abundant dietary fibre. In cultures across Europe, Africa and South America, staple dishes such as millet porridge, barley stews and coarse breads provided a rich tapestry of plant-based nutrition. Even in the UK, just a century ago, working-class diets were dominated by wholegrains and vegetables, with meat as a rare luxury. But after World War II, everything changed.

## MODERN FOOD IS A FIBRE DESERT

Before the 1950s, fibre came built-in to nearly every meal. Today, we've stripped it out, ultra-processed it. The rise of industrial agriculture and food processing transformed what and how we eat. Convenience foods – made with refined sugars and stripped of their natural fibre – replaced the coarse, fibrous staples of the past. Ultra-processed foods (UPFs) such as hyper-palatable packaged snacks, sugary cereals, ready meals and fizzy drinks now account for more than half the calorie intake in both the UK and US[10]. These foods are engineered for taste and shelf life, not nutrition. Bran is removed from grains, skins are peeled off fruits. Legumes such as beans, lentils and chickpeas are replaced with corn or potato starch, guar gum or xanthan gum, leaving us with energy-dense but fibre-poor choices.

Modern agriculture has compounded the problem. Monoculture farming – when a single crop is grown repeatedly on the same land year after year – has become the dominant approach in industrial agriculture. This comes at a cost. It reduces soil microbial diversity and depletes the soil of nutrients, which in turn affects the nutrient and fibre profiles of the crops grown[11].

Chemical fertilization, often used to boost yields in monoculture systems, further disrupts the natural balance of the soil, making it harder for a variety of plants to thrive. As a result, fast-growing, storable and sweet-tasting crops such as wheat, potatoes and corn have replaced their more fibrous ancestors. These modern varieties are bred for uniformity and shelf life, not fibre content or nutritional diversity. Meanwhile, ancient grains such as sorghum, barley, amaranth and rye – once dietary staples and naturally higher in fibre – have been pushed to the margins. This narrowing of crop biodiversity means that the range of fibre-rich foods available in our diets has dramatically decreased, making it even harder to meet our fibre needs through everyday eating.

Lifestyle changes have eroded our fibre intake too. Home-cooked meals with whole ingredients have given way to grab-and-go low-fibre snacks and convenience foods. Even when we do cook, we tend to favour protein and refined carbohydrates over vegetables and legumes.

## THE MEDITERRANEAN EXCEPTION

Some nations, particularly in Southern Europe, have managed to hold on to more traditional eating patterns for longer. Italy, Spain and Greece are renowned for their high consumption of legumes such as beans, lentils and chickpeas, vegetables, fruits, wholegrains, nuts and seeds. Traditional dishes – such as pasta and beans, minestrone, gazpacho and mixed salad – showcase the diversity and richness of plant-based foods. These varied sources of fibre have contributed to lower rates of heart disease, cancers and obesity, when compared to much of Northern Europe. The Mediterranean diet exemplifies balanced nutrition, providing generous amounts of fibre together with a rich array of vitamins, minerals and antioxidants.

However, things are slowly changing here too. The spread of industrial agriculture and ultra-processed foods is gradually leading to less reliance on whole, minimally processed ingredients even in Southern Europe. There has been a noticeable decline in the consumption of traditional fibre-rich foods as modern lifestyles and snacking culture continue to evolve. However, while convenience foods, refined baked goods and sugary cereals are becoming more common, these countries still consume significantly fewer ultra-processed foods than most of the rest of the Western world. For example, UPFs account for only 10–20 per cent of daily calorie intake in Italy, Greece and Spain, compared to more than 50 per cent in countries such as the UK and US[12].

## ACHIEVING OPTIMAL FIBRE INTAKE TODAY

While the traditional Mediterranean diet offers a blueprint for healthy eating, the reality is that most people today struggle to meet recommended fibre intakes. Food manufacturers have responded by adding isolated or synthetic fibres to processed products, but these do not replicate the benefits of fibre found in its natural, whole food context. Whole foods deliver fibre in a nutrient-rich package, working in synergy with antioxidants, vitamins, minerals and water to support digestion, satiety and metabolic health. Processed foods, even those with added fibre, often lack this complexity and can cause digestive discomfort when consumed in excess.

To achieve optimal fibre intake in a modern diet, we need practical solutions to fit both our busy lives and our current food systems. This means finding quick wins: simple changes and easy recipes that make it easier to enjoy fibre-rich meals, even when time and resources are limited. By drawing inspiration from healthier traditional diets and adapting them to today's realities, we can reclaim the benefits of all types of fibre for our gut, metabolism and overall wellbeing.

This book is designed to help you do just that. Here, you'll find easy, delicious recipes that boost fibre intake, inspired by classic dishes from around the world. Whether you're looking for quick breakfasts, hearty lunches or satisfying snacks, these recipes show how simple it can be to enjoy more fibre without sacrificing taste or convenience. Let's rediscover the forgotten macro and make fibre a central part of modern eating.

# THE TRANSITION TO EATING MORE FIBRE

The benefits of eating more fibre include steadier blood sugar, better digestion, happier gut microbes, reduced cholesterol and improved satiety. However, it's important to be aware that adding fibre to your diet can make your body feel different at first. For some, that difference can be bloating, increased wind, a change in stools or a feeling of heaviness after meals. None of this means fibre is 'bad' for you. In fact, the transition symptoms are telling you something useful: that you've changed the food supply in your gut and your microbes are reacting accordingly.

I want to guide you through that transition. By helping you understand what to expect and how to manage the changes, you'll be able to make lasting improvements to your health and experience all the bonuses that a higher-fibre diet can offer.

## WHY THE BODY REACTS TO INCREASED FIBRE

Fibre serves as food for the beneficial bacteria living in your gut. When you increase your fibre intake, these bacteria ferment the fibre, producing gases as natural by-products. This process is similar to how microbes create fermented foods such as sourdough bread, cheese, miso, wine and yogurt. The production of gas is a normal sign that your gut microbes are active and adapting to the new food supply.

If you've been eating a low-fibre diet for a while, your gut microbiome may contain fewer fibre-loving microbes and more bacteria which are used to easy-to-digest simple carbohydrates. Suddenly increasing your fibre intake is like reopening a factory that's been idle. The machinery needs maintenance, the workers have to retrain and new supplies must be sorted and processed. At first, production is noisy and a bit chaotic, but as everyone settles into their roles and the systems adjust, operations become smoother and more efficient! Similarly, your gut microbes need time to adapt, multiply and recalibrate to handle the new workload.

Not everyone will experience digestive symptoms when they increase their fibre intake, but here are the most common, as well as a short explanation of what's behind them. None of them is dangerous in a healthy person and in almost every case they resolve over time.

## Wind & Bloating

Fermentable fibre means fermentation, which results in gas and wind. This often settles after a few days, as microbes adapt.

## Changes in Stool Frequency

More fibre generally means more bulk and softer stools, but the transition period can mean more frequent stools, or, if you don't drink enough water, even the opposite: temporary constipation.

## Cramping or Lower Abdominal Pressure

This can be linked either to fermentation speed, or a sudden increase in the intake of FODMAP-rich foods (see page 37).

## Fullness or Early Satiety

Fibre slows the rate at which your stomach empties. This can be a benefit, as it suppresses appetite, but it can feel surprising when it's new for you.

## Loose Stools

This doesn't happen often, despite what you might have heard, but can occur, especially with soluble fibre, or supplements taken in excess.

## DON'T PANIC!

Western culture tends to treat any digestive symptom as a problem. Feeling bloated or gassy after eating is often treated as a sign that something is 'wrong'. But traditional high-fibre eating cultures have higher fermentation rates and more gas than modern societies, as well as much lower levels of constipation, diverticular disease, metabolic syndrome and inflammatory gut disorders.

Your microbes are meant to be active. Some noise during the transition to eating more fibre is to be expected! In other words: it's normal.

# HOW TO MAKE TRANSITION EASIER

## 1. Go Slow, Really Slow

The biggest mistake is to jump overnight from zero to 25–35g (1–1¼oz) of fibre a day. Instead, go gently. It's worth making a rough estimate of the amount of fibre in your meals, as you start to make the transition. Try to add 3–5g (1⁄16–1⁄8oz) per day each week until you hit your target. This gives both the microbes in your microbiome, and the speed at which your gut empties, time to adjust.

## 2. Drink More Water

Fibre needs water. Without it, stool bulk increases, but softness doesn't. So when you raise the fibre in your diet, increase the amount of water you drink too.

## 3. Be Systematic

At first, start with the easiest to digest forms of fibre, in small portions: oats, chia seeds, cooked vegetables, berries, quinoa, lentils and beans.

Wait a bit for your microbiome to adjust before adding the more challenging types of fibre, found in raw brassicas such as broccoli and cabbage, onions and garlic, salads if you're not used to raw vegetables.

## 4. Go for Cooked Fibre Sources

Cooking partially breaks down plant cell walls. This means less gas and wind and better tolerance of fibre-rich foods. Beans and lentils are easier to digest when well-cooked; easier still for your gut to process if they were pre-soaked before cooking (see pages 40–3).

## 5. Mix Soluble & Insoluble Fibre

Too much insoluble fibre at once can increase stool bulk and speed things up, sometimes a little too quickly. Soluble fibre tempers that, by forming a gel and slowing digestion. This is why combinations such as oats and berries, or beans and rice, work so well together.

## 6. Support Your Microbes

Fermented foods – such as yogurt, kefir, kimchi, sauerkraut or miso – don't replace fibre, but they support your gut during the transition phase by introducing additional microbes. This ensures you have the right beneficial bacteria to process fibre effectively.

## SPECIAL NOTES FOR SENSITIVE GROUPS

### People with IBS

Start with:

- smaller portions of fibre-rich foods

- slower increases in the amount of fibre eaten per day

- lower FODMAP fibre foods first (see page 37)

### People with Chronic Constipation

Drinking more water and eating more soluble fibre often matters more than your intake of insoluble fibre. Psyllium can be an ally (even so, introduce it slowly).

### Older Adults

The time you spend chewing, the amount of water you drink and your mobility will all influence the results of increasing your fibre consumption. Go slowly and prioritize cooked high-fibre foods over raw.

## HOW TO INCORPORATE FIBRE INTO MEALS YOU ALREADY EAT

There are more than 70 recipes in this book that put fibre front and centre. However, it's also easy to make simple swaps to familiar meals, to up their fibre content.

### Upgrade Your Breakfast

- Swap breakfast cereal for oats, buckwheat porridge or pancakes.

- Add chia, flaxseed or berries to yogurt or porridge.

- Choose wholegrain seeded toast with nut butter and fruit.

### Bang in Some Beans

- Toss chickpeas into salads or curries.

- Add brown or green lentils to Bolognese.

- Use black beans in burritos or mixed salad and grain bowls.

### Go Half-and-Half with Grains

If you're used to white rice, pasta, couscous or flour, start mixing in 50 per cent of the wholegrain version. Mix white rice with quinoa, or switch half your white pasta to wholewheat, for instance.

## Sneak in Vegetables Before Dinner

People eat more vegetables if they're hungry. So try an appetizer of raw carrots and hummus, cherry tomatoes and cheese, or cucumber and tahini.

## Garnish with Intent

- Sprinkle sunflower or pumpkin seeds on bowls.
- Add walnuts to porridge.
- Top pasta with rocket.
- Add herbs in handfuls, not pinches.

## Make Snacks Work for You

Don't grab the UPFs. Instead, choose whole foods such as popcorn, nuts and seeds, fruit with nut butter or roasted chickpeas or peas.

## Have a Fast Fibre Stash

Make sure you aways have a fast fibre army stored in your kitchen: chia seeds, flaxseed, oat bran, beans in jars or cans, or frozen berries squirreled away in the freezer.

## Batch-Cook Grains & Legumes

- Lentils to add to soups, stews, salads and wraps.
- Beans to use in tacos, bowls and dips.
- Quinoa or brown rice to use in bowls, stir-fries and breakfasts.

---

### FIVE FIBRE HABITS TO PRACTICE DAILY

**1.** Eat multiple types of vegetable, including roots, members of the cruciferous family such as cauliflower or broccoli and leafy greens like spinach, kale or rocket.

**2.** Include at least one serving of legumes (80g/2¾oz cooked weight), such as lentils, chickpeas or beans.

**3.** Choose wholegrains over the refined varieties.

**4.** Use cooked and cooled starches such as cold toast or reheated potatoes, legumes or pasta, to increase your intake of resistant starch.

**5.** Eat a piece of whole fruit daily, especially apples, pears, a variety of berries or different types of citrus fruit.

---

Remember, every positive change takes a little patience, so stick with it and soon the benefits of a fibre-rich diet will become part of your everyday life.

# GENTLE FIBRE INTRODUCTION MEAL PLAN

Simple ingredient combinations.

| | BREAKFAST | LUNCH | DINNER | |
|---|---|---|---|---|
| **MONDAY** | Cinnamon Multigrain Porridge with Blueberries (page 57) | Sardines & Avocado on Rye (page 83) | Puy Lentil Burgers (page 130) | |
| **TUESDAY** | Kefir Berry Chia Pudding (page 63) | Spiced Lentil & Spinach Soup with High Fibre Bread Roll (pages 81 and 162) | Lean Beef & Rainbow Veggie Stir-fry (page 106) | |
| **WEDNESDAY** | Apple Compote with Yogurt (page 62) | Smoky Smashed Pea Toasts with Egg (page 84) | Tuna & Wholegrain Pasta Bake (page 117) | |
| **THURSDAY** | Nuts & Seeds Granola (page 50) | Tuna & White Bean Salad (page 99) | Salmon with Egg-fried Brown Rice, Spinach & Peas (page 113) | **SNACK** Oat & Almond Energy Bite (page 161) |
| **FRIDAY** | Oat Bran Pancakes with Banana (page 71) | Chicken, Lettuce & Tomato Sandwich (page 87) | Baked Cod with Tomato-Bean Ragù (page 114) | **SIDE** Roasted Carrot & Lentil Mix (page 140) |
| **SATURDAY** | Warm Oat, Walnut, Honey & Pear Bowl with Dark Chocolate (page 60) | Mackerel Grain Bowl (page 100) | Beef, Quinoa & Black Bean Chilli (pages 104–5) | |
| **SUNDAY** | Buckwheat Pancakes with Mushrooms & Cheese (pages 68–9) | Celeriac, Apple, Chestnut & Root Veg Soup with High Fibre Bread Roll (pages 82 and 162) | Smoky Chicken, Lentil & Vegetable Stew (page 109) | **DESSERT** Fudgy Flourless Chocolate Brownies (page 169) |

# QUICK & EASY MEAL PLAN

Recipes that require minimal prep time.

| | BREAKFAST | LUNCH | DINNER | |
|---|---|---|---|---|
| **MONDAY** | Nuts & Seeds Granola (page 50) | Smoky Smashed Pea Toasts with Egg (page 84) | Lean Beef & Rainbow Veggie Stir-fry (page 106) | **SNACK** Pear & Chia Smoothie (page 150) |
| **TUESDAY** | Overnight Oats with Plant-based Protein Powder (page 53) | Chicken, Lettuce & Tomato Sandwich (page 87) | Salmon with Egg-fried Brown Rice, Spinach & Peas (page 113) | **SNACK** Oat & Almond Energy Bite (page 161) |
| **WEDNESDAY** | Kefir Berry Chia Pudding (page 63) | White Bean Feta Salad (page 91) | Chicken Fajita Rice Bowl (page 110) | |
| **THURSDAY** | Cinnamon Multigrain Porridge with Blueberries (page 57) | Tuna & White Bean Salad (page 99) | Chickpea & Spinach Curry (page 118) | **SIDE** Turmeric Roasted Cauliflower (page 145) |
| **FRIDAY** | Carrot & Apple Bircher (page 54) | Spiced Lentil & Spinach Soup (page 81) | Baked Cod with Tomato-Bean Ragù (page 114) | **DESSERT** Fruit & Nut Chocolate Bar (page 172) |
| **SATURDAY** | Warm Oat, Walnut, Honey & Pear Bowl with Dark Chocolate (page 60) | Sardines & Avocado on Rye (page 83) | One-pan Oven Barley Risotto with Mushrooms (page 125) | **SIDE** Roasted Brussels Sprouts with Lemon Tahini Drizzle (page 135) |
| **SUNDAY** | Smashed Avocado on Rye Sourdough (page 66) | Mackerel Grain Bowl (page 100) | Black Bean Tacos (page 126) | **DESSERT** Oat & Nut Crumble with Dark Berries (page 166) |

# MENTAL CLARITY & MOOD SUPPORT MEAL PLAN

Focus on fermented dairy, omega-3 fish, nuts, seeds, legumes.

|  | BREAKFAST | LUNCH | DINNER |  |
|---|---|---|---|---|
| **MONDAY** | Chia Seed Pudding with Dates & Pistachios (page 58) | Roast Carrot Falafel with Citrus Tahini Dressing (page 88) | Salmon with Egg-fried Brown Rice, Spinach & Peas (page 113) |  |
| **TUESDAY** | Nuts & Seeds Granola (page 50) | Apple, Walnut & Blue Cheese Salad with Flaxseed Vinaigrette (page 95) | Kale Pesto with Wholegrain Pasta (page 121) | **SNACK** Green Goddess Smoothie (page 152) |
| **WEDNESDAY** | Kefir Berry Chia Pudding (page 63) | Mackerel Grain Bowl (page 100) | Red Lentil & Coconut Curry (page 122) | **DESSERT** Fruit & Nut Chocolate Bar (page 172) |
| **THURSDAY** | Warm Oat, Walnut, Honey & Pear Bowl with Dark Chocolate (page 60) | White Bean Feta Salad (page 91) | Lean Beef & Rainbow Veggie Stir-fry (page 106) | **SNACK** Berry & Beetroot Smoothie (page 149) |
| **FRIDAY** | Raspberry Chia Jam on Wholegrain Toast (page 75) | Tuna & White Bean Salad (page 99) | Chicken Fajita Rice Bowl (page 110) | **SNACK** Apricot & Oat Brunch Bar (page 159) |
| **SATURDAY** | Carrot & Apple Bircher (page 54) | Curried Roast Butternut Soup with Rye Croutons (pages 78–9) | Beef, Quinoa & Black Bean Chilli (pages 104–5) | **SIDE** Cabbage & Carrot Slaw with Pumpkin Seeds (page 136) |
| **SUNDAY** | Veggie, Egg & Bean Scramble on Wholegrain Toast (page 72) | Barley, Feta & Beetroot Salad (page 92) | Baked Cod with Tomato-Bean Ragù (page 114) | **DESSERT** Berry & Avocado Ice Cream (page 183) |

# HEART HEALTHY MEAL PLAN
## with a particular focus on cholesterol support
Focus on oats, lentils, chickpeas, beans, seeds, oily fish, barley, rye.

| | BREAKFAST | LUNCH | DINNER | |
|---|---|---|---|---|
| **MONDAY** | Cinnamon Multigrain Porridge with Blueberries (page 57) | Tuna & White Bean Salad (page 99) | Chickpea & Spinach Curry (use low-fat coconut milk) (page 118) | **SIDE** Turmeric Roasted Cauliflower (page 145) |
| **TUESDAY** | Carrot & Apple Bircher (page 54) | Sardines & Avocado on Rye (page 83) | Smoky Chicken, Lentil & Vegetable Stew (page 109) | **SNACK** Berry & Beetroot Smoothie (page 149) |
| **WEDNESDAY** | Warm Oat, Walnut, Honey & Pear Bowl with Dark Chocolate (page 60) | Spiced Lentil & Spinach Soup (page 81) | Baked Cod with Tomato-Bean Ragù (page 114) | **SIDE** Easy Tabbouleh (page 139) |
| **THURSDAY** | Overnight Oats with Plant-based Protein Powder (page 53) | Barley, Feta & Beetroot Salad (page 92) | Red Lentil & Coconut Curry (use low-fat coconut milk) (page 122) | **DESSERT** Gluten-free Flaxseed Banana Bread (page 175) |
| **FRIDAY** | Kefir Berry Chia Pudding (page 63) | Curried Roast Butternut Soup with Rye Croutons (pages 78–9) | Salmon with Egg-fried Brown Rice, Spinach & Peas (page 113) | |
| **SATURDAY** | Smashed Avocado on Rye Sourdough (page 66) | Baked Sweet Potato with Black Beans & Avocado (page 96) | Lean Beef & Rainbow Veggie Stir-fry (page 106) | **SIDE** Cabbage & Carrot Slaw with Pumpkin Seeds (page 136) |
| **SUNDAY** | Chickpea Toast with Herbs & Harissa Yogurt (page 65) | Mackerel Grain Bowl (page 100) | White Bean & Feta All-in-One Bake (page 129) | **DESSERT** Oat & Nut Crumble with Dark Berries (page 166) |

# FIBRE MYTHS IN SPECIALIST DIETS

Whichever way you have chosen to eat to best suit your health, both now and in the long-term, fibre will probably be on your radar, and rightly so. Whether you're following keto, paleo, high protein, plant-based or gluten-free diets, fibre should not be overlooked or sacrificed. Careful planning is essential to select fibre sources which align with your chosen dietary approach, ensuring you meet your nutritional needs while supporting your overall health.

However, not everything you might read about fibre's role in the diet you have decided upon rings true to us nutritionists. Let's debunk some of the common myths.

## KETO DIETS

### Myth 1: Fibre will kick you out of ketosis

Reality: Fibre is a carbohydrate, but it's not digested or absorbed as glucose, so it doesn't affect ketosis. Net carbs (total carbs minus fibre) are what matter for ketosis.

### Myth 2: You can't get enough fibre on keto

Reality: With careful planning, keto-friendly fibre sources such as avocados, leafy greens, nuts, seeds, low-carb vegetables and psyllium husk can help meet your fibre needs.

## PALEO DIETS

### Myth 1: Paleo is a meat-only, low-fibre diet

Reality: The paleo diet encourages a variety of fruits, vegetables, nuts and seeds, which are all rich in fibre. The exclusion of grains and legumes does reduce some fibre sources, but a well-planned paleo diet can still be rich in fibre.

### Myth 2: You need grains for fibre

Reality: Many non-grain foods such as berries, root vegetables, leafy greens, nuts and seeds provide both soluble and insoluble fibre. Paleo-friendly fibre sources are abundant, if your diet is varied.

### Myth 3: Fibre is only important for regularity

Reality: Fibre supports blood sugar regulation, cholesterol management and gut health, not just bowel movements.

## HIGH-PROTEIN DIETS

### Myth 1: High-protein diets provide all you need for digestive health

Reality: Focusing on protein often leads to the neglect of fibre-rich foods, resulting in a low fibre intake. Only 5–9 per cent of adults meet fibre recommendations anyway and high-protein diets can decrease your fibre intake.

### Myth 2: Fibre isn't necessary if you're eating enough protein

Reality: Fibre is essential for gut health, blood sugar control and reducing chronic disease risk. High protein, low-fibre diets can cause constipation and gut dysbiosis, as well as increase long-term health risks.

### Myth 3: Animal protein is the only priority

Reality: Plant-based foods are crucial for fibre. A balanced diet should include both protein and fibre sources for optimal health.

---

**GENERAL FIBRE TIPS FOR HIGH-PROTEIN / LOW-CARB DIETS**

- **Add non-starchy vegetables:** Broccoli, spinach, rocket, courgette and cauliflower are low carb but fibre rich.

- **Use seed flours:** Flaxseed, chia and psyllium husk can be baked into breads or crackers.

- **Snack smart:** Olives, nuts and roasted seeds provide fibre.

- **Hydrate well:** When combined, higher fibre and low carbohydrate intake can cause constipation, but drinking plenty of water can balance this out. The non-starchy vegetables, seed flours and smart snack choices outlined above deliver electrolytes – potassium, calcium, sodium and magnesium – to help support this.

## PLANT-BASED & VEGAN DIETS

### Myth 1: All vegan diets are automatically high in fibre

Reality: While plant-based diets tend to be rich in fibre, not all vegan foods are high in fibre. Highly processed vegan foods, such as pastries, white bread or refined grains, can be low in fibre. It's important to choose whole plant foods, such as beans, lentils, wholegrains, fruits and vegetables, to ensure an adequate fibre intake.

### Myth 2: Fibre from plant sources is always sufficient for gut health

Reality: The type and variety of fibre matter. A vegan diet that relies heavily on just one or two fibre sources (such as only oats, or only fruit) may lack the diversity needed for optimal gut health. Rotating sources – choosing every day from beans, peas, oats and vegetables – ensures a mix of soluble and insoluble fibre, which supports a healthy gut microbiome.

### Myth 3: Juices & smoothies provide the same fibre as whole fruits & vegetables

Reality: Juicing removes most of the fibre from fruits and vegetables. Smoothies retain more fibre, but whole forms are best for maximum fibre content. Opting for whole fruit and veg over juice or smoothies is recommended.

---

### GENERAL FIBRE TIPS FOR PLANT-BASED OR VEGAN DIETS

- **Mix legumes & grains:** Pair lentils with brown rice or quinoa for complete protein and fibre.

- **Choose whole forms:** Opt for whole fruit over juice, wholegrains over refined versions.

- **Fortify snacks:** Add chia seeds, flaxseed or hemp seeds to smoothies, porridge or energy bites.

- **Rotate sources:** Variety (beans, peas, oats and veg) ensures a mix of soluble and insoluble fibre.

## GLUTEN-FREE DIETS

### Myth 1: Gluten-free diets are always low in fibre

Reality: While many gluten-free processed foods – such as white rice bread or gluten-free pastries – are low in fibre, a well-planned gluten-free diet can be fibre-rich. Choosing gluten-free wholegrains such as quinoa, buckwheat and brown rice can provide ample fibre.

### Myth 2: You can't get enough fibre without wheat or traditional grains

Reality: There are many naturally gluten-free, fibre-rich foods. Think of legumes, such as lentil pasta, chickpea flour or bean-based dips; seeds such as flax, chia and sunflower; and gluten-free wholegrains. These are all excellent sources of fibre.

### Myth 3: All gluten-free products are healthy & high in fibre

Reality: Many packaged gluten-free products are made with refined flours and starches, which are low in fibre. It's important to check labels for 'wholegrain' and to add vegetables or beans to meals for extra fibre.

---

**GENERAL FIBRE TIPS FOR A GLUTEN-FREE DIET**

- **Choose wholegrains:** Quinoa, buckwheat and brown rice are fibre rich.

- **Add legumes:** Lentil pasta, chickpea flour or bean-based dips add fibre.

- **Seed power:** Flax, chia and sunflower seeds are naturally gluten free and fibre dense.

- **Check labels:** Many GF products are low in fibre, so look for 'wholegrain' on the packet, or add fibre-rich vegetables and beans.

# FIBRE & THE FODMAP DIET

The FODMAP diet is a scientifically supported approach designed to help people with digestive discomfort, such as bloating, pain, or changes in bowel habits, identify foods that may be triggering their symptoms. FODMAPs are specific types of carbohydrates (Fermentable Oligo-, Di-, Monosaccharides, and Polyols) that can be poorly absorbed in the small intestine. This approach has been found to significantly reduce common IBS symptoms like bloating, gas, abdominal pain and diarrhoea by reducing the quantity of these specific carbohydrates which may cause symptoms when they are fermented by gut bacteria in the large intestine.

Many high FODMAP foods e.g. wheat, rye, onions, garlic, legumes and certain fruits are also high in fibre, which can cause confusion. However, plenty of fibre-rich foods are also low in FODMAPs. These include oats, quinoa, chia seeds, carrots, kiwifruit, raspberries, and firm (slightly underripe) bananas, which means it is possible to maintain fibre intake without worsening symptoms.

## GETTING ENOUGH FIBRE ON A LOW FODMAP DIET

Fibre needs can be met on a low FODMAP diet with careful food choices. Support from a FODMAP-trained health professional can help ensure nutritional adequacy and effective symptom management.

## LOWER FODMAP FIBRE OPTIONS

- Oats, quinoa, chia seeds, carrots, kiwifruit, raspberries and firm bananas are gentle on digestion and help maintain fibre intake.

- Almonds, walnuts and flaxseed can be enjoyed in small portions.

- Spinach, courgettes and red peppers are good sources of insoluble fibre and are generally well tolerated.

The FODMAP diet isn't about avoiding fibre, but you do need to work out which fibre sources your digestive system tolerates best while keeping your diet balanced and safe.

# THE HIGH-FIBRE STORE CUPBOARD

As a nutritionist, I see fibre not as a single nutrient to 'get enough of', but as a daily habit. This section is designed to help you adopt that habit, by stocking your cupboards with versatile, fibre-rich staples to support gut health, steady energy levels and improve long-term metabolic wellbeing. I've also included tips on how to cook legumes and brown rice in the most nutritious way, whether using a hob or a pressure cooker.

Here you'll find practical, nourishing staples that fit seamlessly into everyday life. I share my own fibre-rich homemade protein powder, created to boost porridge and smoothies without relying on ultra-processed products, as well as a mixed seed sprinkle to add texture, nourishment and fibre to yogurt, toast or nut butter. You'll also learn how to make a wholegrain, gluten-free flour blend that is significantly higher in fibre than anything commercially available, or a three-grain porridge blend of oats, buckwheat groats and quinoa to keep on hand in the kitchen.

So, because legumes are one of the most powerful and underused sources of fibre, I'll start by guiding you through soaking and cooking them properly.

## COOKING DRIED BEANS, LENTILS & CHICKPEAS

- Always rinse dried legumes.

- Pre-soak all beans and peas in plenty of water (there's no need to soak lentils).

- Consider adding a splash of lemon juice or vinegar to the soaking water, to enhance phytate breakdown (see opposite).

- Discard the soaking water and rinse the beans and peas.

- Cook thoroughly.

- Add salt after cooking, or at the end of cooking, to avoid tough skins.

- If pressure cooking, use Natural Pressure Release (NPR).

- If the peas or beans are not soft enough after pressure cooking and natural pressure release (NPR), simply reseal the pot and cook for a further 5–10 minutes. Older beans will take longer to cook.

- Cooked beans and lentils should hold their shape, but have a little give when pressed between finger and thumb.

- Drain and rinse legumes after cooking.

## WHY SHOULD WE SOAK BEANS & PEAS?

### 1. Reduces Anti-Nutrients (especially Phytates)

Legumes naturally contain phytates, which bind to minerals and reduce how well your body can absorb them. Pre-soaking helps in two ways. It both activates natural enzymes that break down phytates and also allows phytates to leach into the soaking water, which is then discarded.

The minerals most affected are iron, zinc, calcium and magnesium, so soaking beans results in better bioavailability of these, which is especially important for those following plant-based diets.

### 2. Improves Digestibility

Soaking starts the hydration and partial breakdown of complex carbohydrates and proteins.

This makes starches easier for digestive enzymes to access, slightly improves protein digestibility and leads to more even cooking, resulting in less digestive stress and better nutrient utilization.

| | Dry Weight | Water (Hob) | Hob Time | Water (Pressure Cooker) | Pressure Cooker Time |
|---|---|---|---|---|---|
| Chickpeas | 250g (9oz) | 1.5 litres (2½ pints) | 50–60 minutes | 1 litre (1¾ pints) | 18–20 minutes, or 25–30 minutes for very soft beans for hummus or smashed chickpeas (such as for Chickpea Toast with Herbs & Harissa Yogurt, see page 65) |
| White beans | 250g (9oz) | 1.5 litres (2½ pints) | 50–60 minutes (larger beans will need a longer cooking time) | 1 litre (1¾ pints) | 15–18 minutes (larger beans will need a longer cooking time) |
| Green or brown lentils (no soaking required) | 250g (9oz) | 1 litre (1¾ pints) | 25–30 minutes | 750ml (1¼ pints) | 8–10 minutes |
| Black beans | 250g (9oz) | 1.5 litres (2½ pints) | 40–50 minutes | 1 litre (1¾ pints) | 12–14 minutes |

### 3. Reduces Gas-Causing Compounds

Legumes contain oligosaccharides that humans can't digest well. Soaking dissolves a significant portion of these sugars into the water, which means a reduction in fermentation by our gut bacteria after we have eaten the legumes. Naturally, this means less bloating and gas, especially for those with sensitive digestion.

### 4. It's Particularly Beneficial for Certain Groups

Pre-soaking is especially good if you follow a vegetarian or vegan diet, as it helps to maximize mineral absorption (see page 40), which is why it is also great if you have an iron or zinc deficiency. It will help if you experience bloating from legumes, and/or you eat them frequently as a staple protein.

## WHY I RECOMMEND PRESSURE COOKING

Pressure cooking your legumes shortens their cooking time and limits oxygen exposure, so it helps retain heat-sensitive vitamins and minerals that can be lost during a long simmering time on the hob.

## COOKING BROWN RICE

Brown rice is a whole grain, which means it retains its bran and germ, unlike white rice. This makes it richer in fibre and with higher levels of micronutrients including magnesium, iron, and antioxidants.

### • In a Pressure Cooker

For 190g (6½oz) of brown rice, you will need 250ml (9fl oz) of water. Select high pressure for 15 minutes and allow a natural pressure release (NPR) at the end of cooking.

### • On the Hob

For 190g (6½oz) of brown rice, you will need 475ml (17fl oz) of water. Put them both in a saucepan. Bring to a rolling boil, then reduce the heat to low, cover with a tight-fitting lid and simmer gently until cooked through. This should take 25–35 minutes. Fluff up with a fork before serving.

# PLANT-BASED PROTEIN POWDER

Mental Clarity

For Muscle

Vegan

MAKES 15–16 X 30G (1OZ) SCOOPS

100g (3½oz) pumpkin seeds

100g (3½oz) sunflower seeds

75g (2¾oz) chia seeds

35g (1¼oz) milled (ground) flaxseed

110g (4oz) ground almonds

50g (1¾oz) shelled hemp seeds

**All nine essential amino acids in every scoop! You can serve this in your porridge, mix it into nut butter, or blend it into smoothies or smoothie bowls.**

Simply grind all the ingredients together in a food processor until you reach a powder consistency.

Store in a glass jar in the refrigerator and use within 14 days.

per 30g/1oz scoop:

| 167kcal | 13.9g fat | 2.1g sat fat | 6.6g protein | 4g fibre | 0.03g salt |

# MIXED SEED SPRINKLE

## MAKES 13–14 TABLESPOONS

50g (1¾oz) ground flaxseed
50g (1¾oz) shelled hemp seeds
50g (1¾oz) pumpkin seeds
50g (1¾oz) sunflower seeds

**Even just a small amount of this provides you with a combination of soluble and insoluble fibre, plant-based protein and unsaturated fatty acids. Fibre and protein work together to support more stable energy levels and minerals such as magnesium, zinc and iron aid in metabolic and immune function. Meanwhile, omega-3s from flaxseed and hemp contribute anti-inflammatory benefits.**

Simply combine all the seeds in a glass jar with a lid, seal and give the jar a good shake.

Store in the sealed jar in the refrigerator and use within 14 days.

per tablespoon:

| 55kcal | 4.6g fat | 0.03g sat fat | 2.5g protein | 1.2g fibre | 0.01g salt |

# WHOLEGRAIN GLUTEN-FREE FLOUR

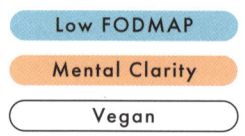

Low FODMAP

Mental Clarity

Vegan

**MAKES 555G (1LB 4OZ)**

255g (9oz) buckwheat flour
150g (5½oz) brown rice flour
75g (2¾oz) arrowroot powder
60g (2¼oz) ground flaxseed

**For the raising agents (optional)**
1 ½ teaspoons bicarbonate
 of soda
1 ½ teaspoons baking powder

This recipe enables you to make the either plain or self-raising flour. Using a higher fibre, higher protein blend in place of standard store-bought gluten-free flour could make all the difference when it comes to the health of your gut. A standard store-bought concoction uses refined flours and gums to bind the mixture, but this wholegrain blend brings much higher levels of fibre and protein without the artificial or ultra-processed additives. For example, one popular store-bought gluten-free self-raising flour brand provides 0.2g (a trace) fibre and 4.6g (⅛oz) protein per 100g (3½oz) flour. This homemade recipe, in contrast, provides 9g (¼oz) fibre and 9.5g (¼oz) protein per 100g (3½oz) flour. The difference is clear.

Simply combine all the ingredients in a jar and shake well to combine.

Keep in an airtight container in a very cool part of your kitchen, or in the refrigerator, and use within 14 days.

per 100g/3½oz:

| 372kcal | 7g fat | 2.5g sat fat | 9.5g protein | 9g fibre | 0.15g salt |

# THREE-GRAIN PORRIDGE BLEND

Low FODMAP

Heart Heathy

Mental Clarity

Vegan

**SERVES 4**

120g (4¼oz) oats
100g (3½oz) buckwheat groats
40g (1½oz) quinoa

One reason why many of us fall short on fibre consumption is that our diets often lack variety, especially when it comes to grains; most people tend to stick to just rice, wheat and corn. This three-grain porridge blend combines a different trio of wholegrains, two of which are complete proteins (meaning they provide all nine essential amino acids). The result is a hearty, satisfying porridge blend that checks all the boxes for nutrition and taste.

While it takes a few extra minutes to prepare compared to regular porridge (see page 57 for my favourite way to cook and serve it), the delicious and nourishing outcome makes it well worth the wait.

Mix together all the grains and store in an airtight jar. It will keep for up to 1 month at room temperature.

To make porridge, see page 57.

per 65g/2½oz:

| 240kcal | 3.5g fat | 0.5g sat fat | 9.8g protein | 6.4g fibre | 0.02g salt |

# BREAKFAST

# NUTS & SEEDS GRANOLA

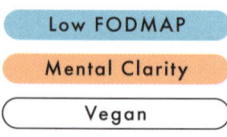

Low FODMAP
Mental Clarity
Vegan

**SERVES 8**

200g (7oz) rolled oats, or jumbo oats

50g (1¾oz) flaked almonds

50g (1¾oz) pecans, roughly chopped

50g (1¾oz) pumpkin seeds

50g (1¾oz) sunflower seeds

2 tablespoons milled (ground) flaxseed

2 tablespoons whole chia seeds

40g (1½oz) toasted coconut flakes

½ teaspoon ground cinnamon

60g (2¼oz) melted coconut oil (about 60ml/4 tablespoons)

4 tablespoons maple syrup, or clear honey

1 teaspoon vanilla extract

40g (1½oz) dried fruit, such as raisins or chopped apricots

Salt

**The combination of toasted coconut, cinnamon and vanilla creates a wonderfully warm, aromatic flavour in this granola, complemented by the crunchy almonds and pecans and the subtle sweetness of maple syrup or honey. It is a fibre-rich blend, designed to support digestive health and keep you fuller for longer.**

Preheat the oven to 170°C, 150°C fan (340°F), Gas Mark 3½. Line a baking tray with baking paper.

In a large bowl, combine the oats, nuts, seeds, coconut flakes, cinnamon and a pinch of salt.

In a separate bowl, mix the oil, maple syrup or honey and vanilla. Pour over the dry mix and stir well. Spread evenly on the prepared tray.

Bake for 20–25 minutes, stirring halfway to bring the toasted edges into the centre, until evenly golden.

Remove from the oven, stir in the dried fruit and let cool completely. The granola will keep in an airtight jar for up to 2 weeks.

Per portion:

| 350kcal | 22g fat | 9.3g sat fat | 9g protein | 10g fibre | 0.2g salt |

# OVERNIGHT OATS WITH PLANT-BASED PROTEIN POWDER

Heart Heathy

For Muscle

Vegetarian

SERVES 1

30g (1oz) Plant-based Protein Powder (see page 44)

30g (1oz) rolled oats

100ml (3½fl oz) semi-skimmed milk

100g (3½oz) natural yogurt

50g (1¾oz) Apple Compote (see page 62)

A powerhouse of a breakfast, combining the goodness of oats with loads of seeds and ground almonds in the protein powder, creamy yogurt and naturally sweet apple purée. Packed with protein and fibre, this jarful will keep you energized and full throughout the morning. Simply mix the ingredients, let them soak overnight, then enjoy a delicious, nutrient-rich breakfast with minimal effort.

Combine all the ingredients in a small glass jar with a lid, then stir well, cover and leave in the refrigerator overnight.

Per portion:

415kcal
20g fat
3g sat fat
19g protein
8g fibre
0.3g salt

# CARROT & APPLE BIRCHER

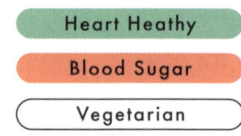

Heart Heathy

Blood Sugar

Vegetarian

## SERVES 2

1 apple, cored and coarsely grated

1 carrot, scrubbed and coarsely grated

50g (1¾oz) rolled oats

20g (¾oz) milled (ground) chia seeds

25g (1oz) flaked almonds

20g (¾oz) raisins, or chopped dried apricots

½–1 teaspoon clear honey, or maple syrup

⅛ teaspoon ground cinnamon

100g (3½oz) natural yogurt

125ml (4fl oz) semi-skimmed milk

A vibrant twist on the classic Swiss breakfast, blending the natural sweetness of apple and carrot with oats, crunchy almonds and chia seeds. Soaked overnight in creamy yogurt and milk, it makes for a delicious mix of flavours and textures. The combination of soluble and insoluble fibres in this Bircher not only aids digestion, but also helps to manage cholesterol and blood sugar.

Combine all the ingredients in a mixing bowl, stir well, then evenly distribute between 2 glass jars with lids.

Cover and leave overnight in the refrigerator.

This will keep, chilled, for up to 3 days.

Per portion:

270kcal    10g fat    2g sat fat    11.5g protein    11g fibre    0.2g salt

# CINNAMON MULTIGRAIN PORRIDGE WITH BLUEBERRIES

**SERVES 1**

65g (2½oz) Three-Grain Porridge Blend (see page 47)
250ml (9fl oz) semi-skimmed milk
60g (2¼oz) blueberries
1 tablespoon almond butter, or peanut butter
¼ teaspoon ground cinnamon
Drizzle of clear honey

A warm, nourishing bowlful that combines three nutritionally varied grains with the natural sweetness of blueberries and a cheerful hint of cinnamon. Using a mix of grains not only boosts the fibre content of this porridge, but also provides a broader spectrum of nutrients, including essential amino acids, vitamins and minerals.

Put the porridge blend in a sieve and rinse well, shake to dry, then tip into a saucepan. Pour in the milk and bring to the boil, then reduce the heat to a simmer, stirring until thickened. This takes 10–15 minutes.

Stir in the blueberries with the almond or peanut butter, cinnamon and honey, then serve.

Per portion:

| 410kcal | 13g fat | 2g sat fat | 14g protein | 8g fibre | 0.2g salt |

# CHIA SEED PUDDING WITH DATES & PISTACHIOS

**SERVES 2**

3 tablespoons chia seeds

250ml (9fl oz) unsweetened plant-based milk

½ teaspoon vanilla extract

1 teaspoon maple syrup (optional)

3 medjool dates, or 2 plump dried figs, finely chopped

2 tablespoons chopped pistachios

Pinch of ground allspice, or ground cardamom

Finely grated zest of 1 orange

Salt

Who says you can't have pudding for breakfast? With plant-based protein and fibre along with the natural sweetness from dates or figs, this recipe is wholesome and satisfying and therefore entirely suitable as the first meal of the day! The pistachios bring a delightful crunch, while orange zest and a hint of allspice or cardamom add a refreshing, aromatic twist.

In a bowl or small jug – to make it easier to pour – mix the chia seeds with the milk, vanilla and a pinch of salt. If you'd like more sweetness, add the maple syrup too. Stir well to prevent clumping, then pour the mixture evenly between 2 glass jars with lids.

Cover and refrigerate for at least 4 hours, or overnight, until thickened.

Before serving, stir in the chopped dates or figs, the pistachios and pinch of spice. Top with the orange zest to serve and enjoy! This will keep in the refrigerator for 3 days.

Per portion:

depending on milk used (soy is higher in protein; almond lower)

| 230kcal | 9g fat | 1g sat fat | 8–10g protein | 8.5–9g fibre | 0.15g salt |

# WARM OAT, WALNUT, HONEY & PEAR BOWL WITH DARK CHOCOLATE

Heart Heathy

Mental Clarity

Anti-inflammatory

Vegan

## SERVES 2

100g (3½oz) rolled oats

500ml (18fl oz) unsweetened oat milk

½ teaspoon ground cinnamon

2 ripe pears, cored and chopped

2 tablespoons chopped walnuts

2 squares of plain dark chocolate

Salt

A comforting combination of creamy oats, juicy pears and crunchy walnuts, all simmered in oat milk. Not only is this delicious and satisfying, but it provides you with a really good portion of dietary fibre from the oats, pears, walnuts and even – would you believe – the dark chocolate. Now that *is* good news...

In a saucepan, combine the oats, oat milk, cinnamon and a pinch of salt. Bring to a gentle simmer.

Add the pears and cook for 7–10 minutes until the oats are creamy and the pears are soft.

Stir in the walnuts and remove from the heat. Divide between bowls and grate the chocolate over the top to serve.

Per portion:

| 320kcal | 10g fat | 1g sat fat | 10g protein | 10.5g fibre | 0.15g salt |

# APPLE COMPOTE WITH YOGURT

Weight Loss

Mental Clarity

Vegetarian

## SERVES 6

8–10 eating apples, cored and chopped into roughly 2cm (¾-inch) cubes

250–300ml (9fl oz–½ pint) water

Juice of ½ lemon

1 teaspoon ground cinnamon

1kg (2lb 4oz) natural yogurt

## Optional higher fibre toppings

Pumpkin or sunflower seeds

Milled (ground) flaxseed

Desiccated coconut

Fresh raspberries

**Apples are rich in both insoluble fibre from their skins, and soluble pectin from their flesh which is particularly beneficial for gut health because it acts as a prebiotic. That means it feeds the beneficial bacteria in your digestive tract, helping to maintain the healthy balance of your gut microbiome, which can support digestion, improve regularity and even contribute to good immune function. Served over creamy natural yogurt, this compote makes for a satisfying breakfast that combines fibre, prebiotics and probiotics, for optimal gut health.**

**This compote freezes beautifully and I always keep portions of it in my freezer, ready to use.**

Simply place the chopped apples in a large saucepan and add about 100ml (3½fl oz) of the measured water. Put the lid on and set over a high heat until some of the liquid is released from the apples. Reduce the heat to a simmer and cook for about 30 minutes, checking regularly and topping up the liquid with splashes of the measured water as needed. You may not need all the water, so bear in mind the consistency you prefer before adding more.

Once all the apples have broken down, you can either use a potato masher to crush it into a purée, or you can pop it into a food processor and blend until smooth. Add the lemon juice and cinnamon, to help both flavour and preserve the purée. The pigments in apple skin may make your compote look pinkish, depending on which variety you use, and this is perfectly normal.

Let cool, then serve over yogurt with any of the optional toppings you like.

## NOTE

If you add 1 tablespoon of each of the suggested optional toppings, the nutritional calculations will increase.

Per portion:

| 220kcal | 5.5g fat | 2g sat fat | 6.5g protein | 4g fibre | 0.15g salt |

# KEFIR BERRY CHIA PUDDING

SERVES 4

85g (3oz) chia seeds

500ml (18fl oz) plain kefir

160g (5¾oz) raspberries

1 tablespoon clear honey

1½ teaspoons toasted coconut flakes

A creamy, probiotic-rich breakfast that combines the gut-friendly benefits of kefir with the fibre and omega-3 of chia seeds. This is a simple and convenient make-ahead option for those busy mornings, as it can be prepped and kept waiting to be grabbed from the refrigerator.

Blend all the ingredients except the coconut in a food processor. Divide evenly between 4 ramekins.

Cover and refrigerate overnight, or for up to 3 days. Serve with the coconut sprinkled on top.

Per portion:

| 197kcal | 10.2g fat | 3g sat fat | 9.8g protein | 11.4g fibre | 0.2g salt |

# CHICKPEA TOAST WITH HERBS & HARISSA YOGURT

Heart Heathy

Mental Clarity

Vegetarian

**SERVES 2**

400g (14oz) can of chickpeas, drained and rinsed

1 tablespoon extra virgin olive oil

½ teaspoon apple cider vinegar

½ teaspoon ground cumin

3 tablespoons chopped parsley leaves

2 slices of wholegrain bread, frozen if possible

3 tablespoons 5 per cent fat Greek yogurt

1 teaspoon harissa paste

Squeeze of lemon juice

Salt and pepper

A delicious savoury breakfast combining hearty smashed chickpeas, parsley and aromatic spice, all finished with a tangy, spicy yogurt topping. It's a quick, satisfying dish bringing together plant-based protein, fibre and bold Mediterranean flavours.

In a bowl with a fork, or in a mini food processor, mash the chickpeas with the oil, vinegar, cumin, parsley, salt and pepper, making sure to leave some texture in the mixture.

Toast the bread until crisp.

Meanwhile, mix the yogurt, harissa and lemon juice together in a small bowl.

Spread the smashed chickpeas generously over each slice of toast and dollop with harissa yogurt. Serve straight away.

Per portion:

| 325kcal | 11.9g fat | 3g sat fat | 10.5g protein | 7.5g fibre | 1.2g salt |

# SMASHED AVOCADO ON RYE SOURDOUGH

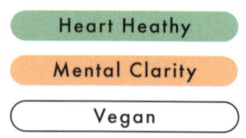

Heart Heathy

Mental Clarity

Vegan

## SERVES 1

2 slices of rye sourdough bread, frozen if possible
1 ripe avocado
Squeeze of lemon juice
Salt and pepper
Chilli flakes, to serve

That earthy tang of rye sourdough bread just works so well with creamy avocado that it has become a modern classic. This simple recipe makes a breakfast rich in fibre, healthy fats and essential nutrients. The toast is brought to life with a squeeze of lemon juice and a sprinkle of chilli flakes, and once you have mastered it, is easy to customize with sliced or pickled vegetables or toasted seeds, such as my Mixed Seed Sprinkle (see page 45).

Toast the rye sourdough slices to your liking.

While the bread is toasting, cut the avocado in half, remove the pit and scoop the flesh into a bowl. Add the squeeze of lemon juice along with a pinch each of salt and pepper, then mash with a fork until you reach your desired texture.

Spread the smashed avocado generously over the toasted rye sourdough.

Top with chilli flakes. Serve immediately and enjoy.

Per portion:

380kcal    22g fat    4g sat fat    9g protein    15-20g fibre    1.9g salt

# BUCKWHEAT PANCAKES WITH MUSHROOMS & CHEESE

Blood Sugar

Mental Clarity

Vegetarian

**SERVES 4**

**For the pancakes**

120g (4¼oz) buckwheat flour

30g (1oz) wholemeal flour, or wholegrain gluten-free flour (for homemade, see page 46)

1 teaspoon baking powder

¼ teaspoon bicarbonate of soda

½ teaspoon salt

1 large egg

240ml (8½fl oz) buttermilk, plus more if needed

2 tablespoons melted butter, cooled

1 teaspoon extra virgin olive oil

**For the topping**

½ tablespoon butter

400g (14oz) sliced mushrooms

120g (4¼oz) Gruyère cheese, vegetarian if needed, grated

Salt and pepper

**Made with buttermilk, fibre-rich buckwheat and wholemeal flours, this is a wholesome and satisfying meal that's ideal for breakfast or brunch. The combination of nutty buckwheat, earthy mushrooms and creamy cheese creates a really comforting start to your day.**

In a bowl, combine the buckwheat flour, wholemeal or wholegrain gluten-free flour, baking powder, bicarbonate of soda and salt. Mix well.

In a separate bowl, lightly beat the egg, then mix in the buttermilk and the cooled melted butter. (The butter mustn't be hot, or the egg might scramble.)

Carefully tip the dry ingredients into the wet ingredients, then stir well to combine. The batter should be thick and smooth, and, when you lift the spoon out of the bowl, it should flow off slowly in a ribbon. If not, then add more buttermilk until you reach this consistency. Leave to settle for 10 minutes before cooking the pancakes.

In a frying pan, heat ½ teaspoon of the extra virgin olive oil. Use a ladle to transfer 1 scoop of batter into the pan. (This amount of batter makes 8 pancakes.) Cook until you see multiple bubbles forming on the surface, then flip and cook the other side. Keep making pancakes until you have used all the batter, using more oil if needed. Set them aside.

Per portion:

| 380kcal | 20g fat | 10g sat fat | 20g protein | 5g fibre | 1.8g salt |

In the same pan, melt the butter and tip in the sliced mushrooms, seasoning well with salt and pepper. Keep stirring until the mushrooms release their liquid and are cooked through; this should take about 10 minutes.

Serve the pancakes with the mushrooms, sprinkling grated Gruyère over the top.

# OAT BRAN PANCAKES WITH BANANA

Mental Clarity

For Muscle

Vegetarian

**SERVES 2**

30g (1oz) oats

30g (1oz) oat bran

3 eggs

100g (3½oz) 5 per cent fat Greek yogurt, plus 2 tablespoons

½ teaspoon olive oil

1 large underripe banana (see recipe introduction)

1 tablespoon desiccated coconut

1 teaspoon maple syrup, or clear honey

Oat bran is a fantastic ingredient for supporting digestive health. It's rich in soluble fibre, particularly beta-glucan, which has been shown to help reduce cholesterol levels, support heart health and promote a feeling of fullness. It also adds a lovely subtle nutty flavour to these pancakes. When selecting a banana, opt for one that's slightly underripe; it should still be palatable, of course, but firmer bananas tend to have significantly more fibre. In fact, an underripe banana can offer one-and-a-half times more fibre than a very ripe one, so that small difference in ripeness makes a big nutritional difference.

Grind the oats and oat bran together in a food processor, then blend in the eggs and the 100g (3½oz) yogurt. Once blended, pour into a bowl and leave to settle for at least 30 minutes.

Heat a frying pan with the olive oil. Scoop one-quarter of the pancake batter into the pan and cook until you see bubbles form on the surface, then flip over and cook the other side. Repeat to make 4 perfectly cooked high-fibre pancakes.

Serve with sliced banana, desiccated coconut, yogurt and maple syrup or honey over the top.

Per portion:

| 384kcal | 17.7g fat | 5g sat fat | 19.7g protein | 7.7g fibre | 0.6g salt |

# VEGGIE, EGG & BEAN SCRAMBLE ON WHOLEGRAIN TOAST

Weight Loss

For Muscle

Vegetarian

## SERVES 2

1 teaspoon olive oil

½ red onion, finely chopped

½ courgette, finely chopped

½ red pepper, finely chopped

400g (14oz) can of cannellini beans, or butter beans, drained and rinsed

3 tablespoons chopped basil leaves

4 large eggs

50g (1¾oz) Parmesan cheese, vegetarian if needed, finely grated

2 slices of wholegrain or seeded bread, frozen if possible

Salt and pepper

There are plenty of examples around the globe of pulses and eggs combining to make a hearty dish: think *huevos rancheros*, the Mexican dish made with eggs, black beans and chillies; Egyptian *ful medames* with hard-boiled eggs; sometimes, even the brunch favourite shakshuka comes with added chickpeas. This recipe is a Mediterranean take on the concept, with eggs scrambled through beans and veggies to make an ideal protein and fibre combo.

Heat the olive oil in a frying pan over medium heat and sauté the onion, courgette and red pepper for 5–7 minutes until soft. Add the beans and basil and cook for 2–3 minutes until the beans are heated through.

Lightly beat the eggs in a bowl with salt and pepper, then pour into the pan and stir gently to scramble, cooking until they are just set. Stir in the cheese at the last minute.

Meanwhile, toast the bread.

Serve the scramble on the toast.

Per portion:

| 550kcal | 23.5g fat | 7g sat fat | 32g protein | 13.5g fibre | 1.6g salt |

# RASPBERRY CHIA JAM ON WHOLEGRAIN TOAST

**MAKES 6 slices**

250g (9oz) frozen raspberries
2 tablespoons chia seeds
1½ tablespoons maple syrup
6 slices of frozen wholegrain
   bread

This jam, naturally sweetened by raspberries and maple syrup, is a good source of fibre, thanks to the berries and chia seeds. Served with hearty wholegrain toast, it's a wholesome breakfast that's easy to prepare, supports digestive health and keeps you feeling satisfied. Plus, freezing your bread before toasting increases its resistant starch content, offering even more health benefits.

Simply heat the frozen berries over a medium heat in a small saucepan, stirring occasionally. They will reduce and start to look jammy in consistency after 5–10 minutes. Remove from the heat, add the chia seeds and maple syrup, then leave to cool fully.

Meanwhile, sterilize a jam jar. Preheat the oven to 140°C, 120°C fan (275°F), Gas Mark 1. Wash the jar in hot soapy water, rinse well, place on a baking sheet and put into the oven for about 10 minutes. Leave to cool to room temperature.

Decant the cooled jam into the cooled sterilized jam jar and keep in the refrigerator for up to 1 week.

When you're ready for breakfast, remove the bread slices from the freezer and toast to your liking. Serve with the chia jam spread on top.

## NOTE

If you're looking to boost both satisfaction and nutrition, you could add a second slice of wholegrain toast to your plate, topped with 1 tablespoon almond butter and 1 tablespoon shelled hemp seeds. It is delicious and it packs an impressive 10.5g (¼oz) protein per slice, along with an extra 7g (⅛oz) fibre.

per slice:

| 140kcal | 3g fat | 0.7g sat fat | 4g protein | 8.5g fibre | 0.4g salt |

# LUNCH

# CURRIED ROAST BUTTERNUT SOUP WITH RYE CROUTONS

Heart Heathy

Weight Loss

Vegan

**SERVES 4**

1 tablespoon olive oil

1 onion, finely chopped (or see recipe introduction)

2 carrots, finely chopped (or see recipe introduction)

2 celery sticks, finely chopped (or see recipe introduction)

3 garlic cloves, chopped

5cm (2-inch) piece of fresh root ginger, chopped

250g (9oz) split yellow peas, rinsed and drained

1.6 litres (3 pints) vegetable stock, made from 3 stock cubes

2 teaspoons mild curry powder

¾ teaspoon ground turmeric

1 teaspoon nigella seeds

¾ teaspoon ground cumin

Juice of ½ lemon

Salt and pepper

**For the croutons**

2 thick slices of rye bread, in 2.5cm (1-inch) cubes (use unsliced wholemeal bread if you cannot find unsliced rye in the shops)

1 tablespoon olive oil

Split yellow peas give creamy texture to this aromatic soup with its crunchy rye croutons; a great mix of soluble and insoluble fibre. The croutons provide both texture and extra fibre, while the gentle spices and lemon juice add a zingy lift. A warming bowlful, perfect for chilly days.

To make the recipe near effort-free, substitute 300g (10½oz) fresh or frozen ready-prepared soffritto or vegetable base mix (both names for the same product) for the chopped onion, carrots and celery: a combination of the same vegetables, that you can buy in the supermarket.

In a large saucepan, heat the olive oil over a medium heat. Add the onion, carrots and celery and sauté for 8–10 minutes until softened but without colour. Add the garlic and ginger and cook for 1 minute more.

Stir in the split yellow peas, stock and spices. Bring to the boil, then reduce the heat to low. Simmer for 45–55 minutes, stirring occasionally, until the peas break down and become creamy.

Meanwhile, preheat the oven to 220°C, 200°C fan (425°F), Gas Mark 7.

Toss the squash cubes with the olive oil, salt and pepper. Spread on a baking sheet in a single layer and roast for 25–30 minutes until caramelized and tender.

Toss the rye bread cubes in the oil and a little salt, lay them in a single layer on a baking sheet and bake alongside the squash for 10–12 minutes or until crisp.

Per portion:

| 425kcal | 11g fat | 1.65g sat fat | 10g protein | 10.5g fibre | 3g salt |

### For the squash

1 small butternut squash, peeled, deseeded and cubed (total weight about 300g/10½oz)

1 tablespoon olive oil

½ teaspoon sea salt

¼ teaspoon pepper

Add the roasted squash to the pan and simmer for a final 10 minutes to meld the flavours. For a smooth soup, blend in a blender or food processor, or with a stick blender. Stir in the lemon juice, then taste and adjust the salt and pepper, if needed.

Serve the soup in warmed bowls, scattered with the rye croutons.

# SPICED LENTIL & SPINACH SOUP

**SERVES 4**

1 tablespoon extra virgin olive oil

2 onions, finely chopped (or see recipe introduction)

2 carrots, finely chopped (or see recipe introduction)

2 celery sticks, finely chopped (or see recipe introduction)

2 garlic cloves, finely chopped

1 teaspoon ground cumin

½ teaspoon ground coriander

150g (5½oz) split red lentils, rinsed and drained

1.2 litres (2 pints) vegetable stock, made from 2½ stock cubes

2 large handfuls of spinach or kale, coarse stalks removed

Juice of ½ lemon

Salt and pepper

> ## NOTE
> To increase the protein available from this soup, serve it with a dollop of Greek yogurt (4–5g/⅛oz protein), 2 tablespoons toasted pumpkin seeds (4.5g/⅛oz protein), Mixed Seed Sprinkle (2.5g/¹⁄₁₆oz protein, see page 45), a slice of wholegrain bread (4–5g/⅛oz protein) or a few cubes of cheese (about 5g/⅛oz protein), or a combination of these.

The perfect, nutrient-packed comfort food for any season. Gentle spices enhance the soup's flavour, while fibre-rich lentils and antioxidant-packed green veg ensure each bowl is truly nourishing.

As before (see page 78), you can substitute the onions, carrots and celery for 300g (10½oz) ready-prepared soffritto or vegetable base mix, to save time.

Set a large saucepan with the extra virgin olive oil over a medium-high heat, then sauté the onions, carrots, celery and garlic for about 5 minutes, or until softened but without colour. Add the spices, lentils and stock.

Bring to the boil, then reduce the heat to a simmer and cook for 25 minutes.

Add the spinach or kale and cook until wilted, then squeeze in the lemon juice.

Blend using a stick blender, or leave chunky, then taste and adjust the seasoning before serving in warmed bowls.

**Per portion:**

| 213kcal | 4.5g fat | 1.2g sat fat | 4.5g protein | 5.5g fibre | 2.75g salt |

# CELERIAC, APPLE, CHESTNUT & ROOT VEG SOUP

Weight Loss

Anti-inflammatory

Vegan

## SERVES 4

1½ teaspoons olive oil

½ onion, chopped (or see recipe introduction)

1 carrot, chopped (or see recipe introduction)

1 celery stick, chopped (or see recipe introduction)

1 garlic clove, chopped

½ teaspoon dried thyme

225g (8oz) peeled and chopped celeriac

½ large parsnip, scrubbed and chopped

125g (4½oz) scrubbed and chopped sweet potato

1 apple, cored and chopped

750ml (1¼ pints) vegetable stock, made from 1½ stock cubes

100g (3½oz) ready-made chestnut purée

Salt and pepper

A lovely seasonal midwinter bowlful, with the subtle tartness of apple and the richness of chestnut purée doing wonders for the flavour and texture. This recipe, using simple ingredients, is ideal for anyone looking to boost their fibre intake during the colder months.

As before (see page 78), you can substitute the onion, carrot and celery for 125g (4½oz) ready-prepared soffritto or vegetable base mix, to save time.

Heat the olive oil in a large saucepan over a medium heat and sauté the onion, carrot and celery for 5 minutes, or until softened but without colour. Add the garlic and thyme and cook for 1 minute.

Now tip in all the chopped root vegetables and stir to coat them in the flavourings. Add the apple, then pour in the stock. Bring to the boil, then simmer for 30 minutes or until all the vegetables are tender (check a larger piece of celeriac with a knife: it should meet no resistance).

Turn off the heat, stir in the chestnut purée and allow the soup to cool a little, then blend until smooth using a stick blender or food processor. Serve in warmed bowls.

## NOTE

To increase the fibre and protein of this lunch, serve it with crackers and hummus, or with a slice of Sardines & Avocado on Rye (see page 83).

Per portion:

141kcal     2.5g fat     0.7g sat fat     2g protein     4.5g fibre     1.5g salt

# SARDINES & AVOCADO ON RYE

Blood Sugar

Mental Clarity

**SERVES 2**

2 slices of rye bread, frozen if possible

1 avocado, pitted and peeled

8 cornichons or mini gherkins, or 4 gherkin slices

120g (4¼oz) can of sardines in oil, drained

Salt and pepper

**Sardines are an excellent lunch, waiting in their can in the kitchen cupboard for weeks until you're ready for their protein-and-omega-3-rich deliciousness. When you add tangy pickles and a bed of classic avocado and rye, this makes for a splendid and nutrient-dense meal.**

Toast the rye bread.

Meanwhile, mash the avocado in a bowl with a fork and add salt and pepper, about ⅛ teaspoon of each.

Top the toast with the mashed avocado and the cornichons or gherkins, then arrange the sardines on top and eat straight away.

Per portion:

| 285kcal | 3.5g fat | 16.5g sat fat | 14g protein | 8g fibre | 2g salt |

# SMOKY SMASHED PEA TOASTS

**SERVES 2**

200g (7oz) frozen peas

4 slices of wholegrain or seeded bread, frozen if possible

1 tablespoon olive oil

Squeeze of lemon juice

1 teaspoon smoked paprika, sweet or hot, as you prefer

Salt and pepper

**For the eggs (optional)**

2 teaspoons extra virgin olive oil

4 eggs

**Bright, fresh and packed with flavour, this is a ridiculously simple yet satisfying light lunch made from store cupboard ingredients. The peas are seasoned with lemon juice and smoked paprika and generously spread over toasted wholegrain bread. For extra richness and protein, crispy fried eggs can be added on top: either way, this is a delicious recipe.**

Boil or steam the peas for 3–4 minutes until tender. Drain well and tip into a bowl.

If you are cooking the eggs, heat the olive oil in a frying pan. Crack in the eggs and fry until crispy and frilly.

Toast the bread.

Mash the drained peas with a fork or potato masher, leaving some texture (don't purée completely). Stir in the oil, lemon juice, paprika, salt and pepper. Spread the smashed peas generously over the toasts. Top each slice with a crispy fried egg, if you like, and serve straight away.

Per portion (with eggs):

| 420kcal | 24g fat | 5g sat fat | 23g protein | 8g fibre | 2.6g salt |

# CHICKEN, LETTUCE & TOMATO SANDWICH

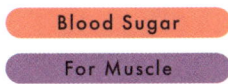

Blood Sugar
For Muscle

**SERVES 2**

4 slices of wholegrain or seeded bread

1 avocado, pitted, peeled and mashed

2 tablespoons hummus

4–6 crisp lettuce leaves, such as little gem

2 tomatoes, sliced

150g (5½oz) cooked chicken breast, sliced or shredded

Pepper

This seemingly simple sandwich is designed to contain hidden healthy fats and extra fibre from the avocado and hummus, but with no extra effort on your part. A wholesome and satisfying combination of lean protein, vegetables and high-fibre wholegrain bread. Serve with a side of carrot sticks and/or apple slices for extra crunch and fibre.

Lightly toast the slices of bread. Spread the mashed avocado over 2 of the slices, then the hummus. Add the lettuce leaves, then the tomato slices.

Layer on the chicken and season with pepper, then top each stack with the remaining toasts. Slice and serve.

Per portion:

430kcal · 16g fat · 3g sat fat · 25g protein · 13g fibre · 1.25g salt

# ROAST CARROT FALAFEL WITH CITRUS TAHINI DRESSING

Mental Clarity
Anti-inflammatory
Vegan

## MAKES 10 / SERVES 2

2 carrots, scrubbed, cut into 1.5cm (5/8-inch) cubes (total weight about 200g / 7oz)

2 tablespoons olive oil, plus more for baking

400g (14oz) can of butter beans, drained and rinsed

1 small red onion, very finely chopped

1 teaspoon ground cumin

¾ teaspoon ground coriander

½ teaspoon smoked paprika, hot or sweet, as you prefer

2 tablespoons chopped parsley leaves

2 tablespoons milled (ground) flaxseed

1 tablespoon wholemeal flour, or Wholegrain Gluten-Free Flour (see page 46) (optional)

Salt and pepper

### For the dressing

30g (1oz) tahini

1 tablespoon orange juice

2 teaspoons apple cider vinegar

1 teaspoon maple syrup

1 teaspoon water (optional)

A twist on a classic, these falafel are made with creamy butter beans rather than the traditional chickpeas. Butter beans provide a smooth texture and mild flavour that works well with the sweetness of the roast carrots. These falafel are crisp on the outside, soft on the inside and paired with a tangy, protein-rich sauce.

Preheat oven to 200°C, 180°C fan (400°F), Gas Mark 6. Line a baking tray with baking paper.

Toss the carrot cubes into another baking tray with 2 teaspoons of the olive oil, salt and pepper. Roast for 30 minutes, or until tender and lightly caramelized. Increase the oven temperature to 220°C, 200°C fan (425°F), Gas Mark 7.

In a food processor, combine the roasted carrots, beans, onion, spices, parsley, flaxseed and remaining 4 teaspoons of olive oil, seasoning well. Pulse until the mixture is coarse but holds together. Add the flour, if needed, to firm up the texture.

Scoop tablespoons of the mixture and shape it into 10 small balls. Place on the prepared baking tray, then gently flatten each with your hand or the back of a fork. Drizzle over a little olive oil.

Bake for 30–35 minutes, turning halfway, until golden and crisp on the outside but soft on the inside.

Meanwhile, combine all the ingredients for the dressing, except the water, in a glass jar with a lid, adding a good pinch of salt. Secure the lid and shake well, add the water if you need a looser texture and shake again, then serve over or alongside the falafel.

Per portion:

| 320kcal | 15g fat | 3.1g sat fat | 12g protein | 13g fibre | 2.1g salt |

# WHITE BEAN FETA SALAD

**SERVES 4**

80g (2¾oz) walnuts

2 x 400g (14oz) cans of butter beans, drained and rinsed

80g (2¾oz) baby spinach

12 cherry tomatoes, halved

1 banana shallot, halved and very thinly sliced

3 tablespoons chopped dill

250g (9oz) feta cheese, vegetarian if needed, crumbled

### For the dressing

2 tablespoons lemon juice

½ tablespoon clear honey

2 tablespoons 5 per cent fat Greek yogurt

50ml (1¾fl oz) extra virgin olive oil

½ teaspoon Dijon mustard

1 small garlic clove, grated (optional)

Salt and pepper

**Escape to the Mediterranean at lunchtime, with this Med-inspired dish of aromatic dill, tangy feta and crunchy toasted walnuts. It's a vibrant, refreshing and satisfying salad, just perfect for lunch.**

Dry-fry the walnuts in a frying pan for 3–5 minutes, shaking the pan at regular intervals. Remove from the pan to cool, then chop the nuts.

Put all the ingredients for the dressing into a jar with a lid and season well. Secure the lid and shake well to combine.

Toss all the salad ingredients, except the walnuts, into a large bowl and coat with the dressing. Top with the walnuts and serve immediately.

Per portion:

| 645kcal | 35g fat | 10.4g sat fat | 22g protein | 10g fibre | 2.3g salt |

# BARLEY, FETA & BEETROOT SALAD

Heart Heathy

Weight Loss

Anti-inflammatory

Vegetarian

## SERVES 4

185g (6½oz) pearl barley
250g (9oz) cooked beetroot
2 tablespoons extra virgin
olive oil
1 tablespoon clear honey
1 tablespoon balsamic vinegar
20g (¾oz) pine nuts
20g (¾oz) pistachios
125g (4½oz) feta cheese,
vegetarian if needed, crumbled
10 green pitted olives, halved
3 tablespoons mint leaves, torn
Salt and pepper

Nutty pearl barley makes an intriguing change to blander salad grains such as quinoa, and is so satisfying that it's easy to understand why it was traditionally so popular for bulking out stews and soups. When it's combined with sweet beetroot, creamy feta, pine nuts, pistachios and mint leaves and finished with a honey-balsamic dressing and olives, it's not hard to see why this filling, nutritionally balanced and fibre-rich recipe will remain firmly in your regular lunch repertoire.

Rinse the barley and boil for 25–35 minutes in well-salted water until the grains are plump and cooked. Taste the barley from about 25 minutes, to check if it's cooked. Once ready, strain, rinse and cool, then return to its empty saucepan.

Grate the beetroot.

In a small jar with a lid, combine the oil, honey and balsamic vinegar with a little salt and pepper. Secure the lid and shake well to mix. Add this dressing to the boiled barley with the grated beetroot and stir gently, then transfer to a serving bowl. Leave to chill in the refrigerator for 1 hour before serving.

Meanwhile, dry-fry the pine nuts and pistachios in a frying pan for 2–4 minutes to colour, shaking regularly. Tip on to a plate and leave to cool a little, then chop.

Serve the barley and beetroot with the crumbled feta, toasted nuts, olives and mint scattered over the top.

Per portion:

| 410kcal | 21g fat | 5.6g sat fat | 11.5g protein | 6.5g fibre | 1.5g salt |

# APPLE, WALNUT & BLUE CHEESE SALAD WITH FLAXSEED VINAIGRETTE

Blood Sugar
Anti-inflammatory
For Muscle
Vegetarian

### SERVES 2

40g (1½oz) walnuts

1 tablespoon pumpkin seeds

100g (3½oz) mixed leafy greens, such as baby spinach, rocket or watercress

2 apples, thinly sliced

½ small red onion, thinly sliced (optional)

50g (1¾oz) celery sticks, thinly sliced

2 tablespoons dried cranberries, or raisins

100g (3½oz) soft blue cheese such as Roquefort, vegetarian if needed

### For the vinaigrette

2 tablespoons milled (ground) flaxseed

3 tablespoons extra virgin olive oil

2 tablespoons apple cider vinegar

¾ teaspoon Dijon mustard

1 teaspoon clear honey

Salt and pepper

**A delightful blend of crisp apples, toasted walnuts and creamy blue cheese, all tossed with mixed leafy greens and a tangy vinaigrette. Pumpkin seeds, dried cranberries and celery bring extra texture and flavour.**

Dry-fry the walnuts and pumpkin seeds in a frying pan over a medium heat for 3–4 minutes until fragrant, shaking the pan regularly. Tip on to a plate and set aside to cool.

In a small jar with a lid, combine all the dressing ingredients, seasoning well. Secure the lid and shake well to blend.

In a large bowl, combine the leafy greens, apples, onion, if using, celery, cranberries or raisins, toasted walnuts and pumpkin seeds and toss gently with the flaxseed vinaigrette. Crumble over the blue cheese just before serving.

Per portion:

| 720kcal | 55g fat | 12g sat fat | 19g protein | 10g fibre | 2g salt |

# BAKED SWEET POTATO WITH BLACK BEANS & AVOCADO

Weight Loss

Anti-inflammatory

Vegan

## SERVES 2

2 sweet potatoes

1 tablespoon olive oil

1 small red onion, finely chopped

1 garlic clove, minced

400g (14oz) can of black beans, drained and rinsed

1 teaspoon ground cumin

½ teaspoon smoked paprika, hot or sweet, as you prefer

1 small lime

1 ripe avocado, pitted, peeled and chopped

Salt and pepper

Handful of coriander, chopped, to serve

If you're at home and can manage to pop the sweet potatoes in the oven an hour ahead of lunchtime, this is a smart choice for time-poor people looking to boost their fibre intake in the middle of the day. Zesty lime and fragrant coriander really lift the flavours, while the dramatic black and orange colours make a cheerful canvas on the plates.

Preheat the oven to 200°C, 180°C fan (400°F), Gas Mark 6. Scrub the sweet potatoes, prick them with a fork, then bake on a tray for 40–50 minutes until tender.

Heat the olive oil in a frying pan and sauté the onion for 5 minutes until softened. Add the garlic, black beans, cumin, paprika, salt and pepper and cook for 5–7 minutes, stirring occasionally. If the beans are starchy and start to stick, then add a dash of water. Turn off the heat and squeeze in the juice of half the lime.

Slice the baked sweet potatoes open lengthways and spoon in the black bean mixture. Top with chopped avocado and serve scattered with coriander, with lime wedges on the side.

Per portion:

| 520kcal | 22g fat | 1.4g sat fat | 11g protein | 18g fibre | 0.45g salt |

# TUNA & WHITE BEAN SALAD

## SERVES 2

400g (14oz) can of white beans, such as butter beans, drained and rinsed

160g (5¾oz) can of tuna in spring water, drained and broken into smaller chunks

½ red onion, finely chopped

1 large tomato, deseeded and chopped

2 tablespoons basil leaves

### For the dressing

1 tablespoon lemon juice

2 tablespoons extra virgin olive oil

½ teaspoon Dijon mustard

½ teaspoon clear honey

Salt and pepper

**An ideal pairing: mild, creamy white beans balance savoury tuna and they both absorb the dressing beautifully. The beans are an excellent source of dietary fibre, which complements the protein from tuna, creating a nutrient-rich lunch.**

Place all the salad ingredients into a serving bowl.

Combine the dressing ingredients in a small jar with a lid, seasoning well. Secure the lid and shake well.

Gently toss the salad in the dressing until well combined, then serve immediately.

Per portion:

| 380kcal | 15.75g fat | 2.3g sat fat | 34g protein | 11g fibre | 1.1g salt |

# MACKEREL GRAIN BOWL

**SERVES 4**

85g (3oz) pearl barley (or see recipe introduction)

2 smoked mackerel fillets, skin removed, flesh flaked

100g (3½oz) cooked Puy lentils

1 large avocado, pitted, peeled and cubed

1 apple, cored and cubed

Seeds of ½ pomegranate (total weight about 100g/3½oz)

3 tablespoons pumpkin seeds

30g (1oz) baby spinach

**For the dressing**

Juice of ½ lemon

1 tablespoon extra virgin olive oil

1 teaspoon balsamic vinegar

Salt and pepper

A nutrient-dense meal delivering a balance of protein, healthy fats and dietary fibre. To make life even easier at lunchtime, you could also use 250g (9oz) ready-cooked pearl barley rather than cooking your own. Pomegranate seeds lend a festive edge and make the bowls look like the special treat they are.

Rinse the barley and boil for 25–35 minutes in well-salted water until the grains are plump and cooked. Taste the barley from about 25 minutes, to check if it's cooked. Once ready, strain, rinse and cool.

In a bowl, combine the cooked barley, flaked fish, lentils, avocado, apple, pomegranate seeds, pumpkin seeds and spinach.

Combine all the dressing ingredients in a small glass jar with a lid. Seal the lid and shake well to combine, then stir into the salad ingredients and serve.

Per portion:

| 320kcal | 17g fat | 3.1g sat fat | 15g protein | 9g fibre | 1.3g salt |

# DINNER

# BEEF, QUINOA & BLACK BEAN CHILLI

Weight Loss

Blood Sugar

For Muscle

## SERVES 6

1 tablespoon olive oil

1 onion, finely chopped (or see recipe introduction)

1 carrot, finely chopped (or see recipe introduction)

1 celery stick, finely chopped (or see recipe introduction)

2 garlic cloves, minced

1 red pepper, finely chopped

500g (1lb 2oz) lean minced beef

1 teaspoon ground cumin

1 teaspoon smoked paprika, sweet or hot, as you prefer

1 teaspoon chilli powder, or to taste

150g (5½oz) quinoa, rinsed and drained

400g (14oz) can of chopped tomatoes

1 tablespoon Worcestershire sauce

2 tablespoons tomato purée

400g (14oz) can of black beans, drained and rinsed

100g (3½oz) canned or frozen sweetcorn

500ml (18fl oz) vegetable stock, made from 1 stock cube

Salt and pepper

A hearty, nourishing twist on a classic chilli con carne. By adding quinoa, which is a protein-rich pseudo-grain, and black beans, this version delivers a serious boost of fibre, plant protein and slow-release energy. The quinoa helps create a satisfying yet almost 'meaty' texture while the beans bring depth and creaminess. Finish this dish with fresh coriander, creamy avocado and a light sprinkle of cheese for balance. It's a vibrant, nutrient-dense chilli that's comforting, super filling and naturally supportive of steady blood sugar.

**To speed up the recipe, you can substitute the onion, carrot and celery for 175g (6oz) fresh or frozen ready-prepared soffritto or vegetable base mix (see page 78).**

Heat the olive oil in a large saucepan over a medium heat. Add the onion, carrot, celery, garlic and red pepper. Cook for 5–6 minutes until softened, but without colour.

Add the minced beef, breaking it up with a spoon, and cook, stirring and breaking the meat up, until browned on all sides.

Stir in the cumin, paprika and chilli powder. Add the quinoa, tomatoes, Worcestershire sauce, tomato purée, black beans, sweetcorn and stock. Season, stir well, bring to the boil, then reduce the heat to a simmer.

Per portion (with all the optional toppings):

| 601kcal | 35g fat | 13g sat fat | 29.7g protein | 9.4g fibre | 1.6g salt |
|---------|---------|-------------|---------------|------------|-----------|

**To serve (optional)**

20g (¾oz) plain dark chocolate, grated (adds both flavour and fibre)

2 avocados, pitted, peeled and sliced

80g (2¾oz) grated Red Leicester cheese, or similar

Handful of coriander, roughly chopped

Cook uncovered for 25–30 minutes until the quinoa is tender and the chilli thickens. Taste and adjust the seasoning with salt and pepper as needed.

Ladle into warmed bowls and serve, with the grated dark chocolate, sliced avocados, grated cheese and coriander, if you like.

# LEAN BEEF & RAINBOW VEGGIE STIR-FRY

Blood Sugar

For Muscle

## SERVES 2

1 tablespoon sesame oil, or olive oil

375g (13oz) lean beef strips

2 garlic cloves, finely chopped

5cm (2-inch) piece of fresh root ginger, finely chopped

½ red chilli, finely chopped

1 red pepper, sliced

1 yellow pepper, sliced

1 small head of broccoli, cut into florets

1 carrot, very thinly sliced

1 small courgette, cut into matchsticks

50g (1¾oz) green beans, topped, tailed and halved

¼ teaspoon 5 spice

2 tablespoons soy sauce, plus more if needed

1 tablespoon rice vinegar

1 tablespoon clear honey

2 tablespoons water

## To serve

200g (7oz) cooked brown rice

1 tablespoon sesame seeds

Handful of chopped coriander, or sliced spring onion

**Quick to prepare and perfect for a balanced weeknight dinner. This is an excellent recipe to use when you want to clear out the vegetable drawer, so feel free to substitute the vegetables listed here for what you have, suitably sliced or chopped. Just make sure there's a good variety.**

Heat the oil in a large wok or frying pan over a high heat. Add the beef strips and stir-fry for 2–3 minutes until browned. Remove and set aside.

Add the garlic, ginger and chilli to the pan, immediately followed by all the vegetables. Stir-fry for 1 minute, then add the 5 spice, soy sauce, rice vinegar, honey and measured water and place a lid over the pan. Steam-fry the veg, stirring occasionally, for 5–10 minutes until the broccoli floret stems are just softened.

Return the beef to the pan and stir well to coat it in the flavourings. Cook for another 2 minutes until heated through.

Check the seasoning and add more soy sauce if necessary. Serve over brown rice, sprinkled with sesame seeds and coriander or spring onion.

> ### NOTE
> Here are four easy ways to boost the fibre content of your weekly stir-fry:
> Include some broccoli stalk, finely sliced into thin matchsticks; depending how much you use, this could add 1–3g fibre.
> Serve over wholewheat noodles or quinoa, to add 2–4g fibre per 100g (3½oz) used.
> Sprinkle over toasted pumpkin or sunflower seeds, or my Mixed Seed Sprinkle (see page 45), to add 1g fibre per tablespoon used.
> Add edamame beans and/or frozen peas to add 2–3g fibre per 50g (1¾oz) used.

Per portion:

| 550kcal | 20g fat | 6.6g sat fat | 36g protein | 8.9g fibre | 3g salt |

# SMOKY CHICKEN, LENTIL & VEGETABLE STEW

**SERVES 4**

1 tablespoon olive oil

1 onion, finely chopped (or see recipe introduction)

1 carrot, finely chopped (or see recipe introduction)

1 celery stick, finely chopped (or see recipe introduction)

2 garlic cloves, finely chopped

500g (1lb 2oz) skinless boneless chicken thighs, cut into bite-sized pieces

1 teaspoon smoked paprika, hot or sweet, as you prefer

1 teaspoon ground cumin

1 teaspoon sea salt

150g (5½oz) green lentils, rinsed

1 courgette, chopped

1 head of broccoli, chopped into florets

400g (14oz) can of chopped tomatoes

2 tablespoons tomato purée

750ml (1¼ pints) vegetable stock, made from 1½ stock cubes

Juice of 1 lemon

Handful of parsley leaves, chopped

Pepper

4 thick slices of wholegrain bread, to serve (optional)

A reassuring meal that delivers a comforting warmth, flavoured with smoked paprika, cumin and a splash of lemon juice. It pairs beautifully with wholegrain bread for extra fibre, and, of course, for mopping up all the flavourful juices.

You can substitute the onion, carrot and celery for 175g (6oz) fresh or frozen ready-prepared soffritto or vegetable base mix (see page 78).

This works well as a meal with Roasted Brussels Sprouts with Lemon Tahini Drizzle (see page 135).

Heat the olive oil in a large saucepan over a medium heat. Add the onion, carrot, celery and garlic and cook for 5–6 minutes until softened, but without colour.

Stir in the chicken pieces, paprika, cumin and salt and cook until the chicken is lightly browned on all sides.

Add the lentils, courgette, broccoli, chopped tomatoes, tomato purée and stock. Bring to the boil, then reduce the heat to a gentle simmer.

Cook uncovered, for 30–35 minutes until the lentils are tender and the chicken is cooked through. Add the lemon juice and adjust the seasoning with pepper, if needed.

Ladle into warmed bowls, scatter with the parsley and serve with wholegrain bread, if you like.

Per portion (with wholegrain bread):

| 610kcal | 17.5g fat | 3.5g sat fat | 38.5g protein | 11g fibre | 2.9g salt |

# CHICKEN FAJITA RICE BOWL

**SERVES 4**

1 red pepper, sliced

1 yellow pepper, sliced

1 red onion, sliced into wedges

400g (14oz) skinless, boneless chicken thighs, roughly chopped

1½ tablespoons fajita seasoning, shop-bought or homemade (see below)

2 tablespoons olive oil

150g (5½oz) cooked black beans

200g (7oz) cooked brown rice

Juice of 1 lime, plus wedges to serve

3 tablespoons chopped coriander, plus more to serve

1 avocado, pitted, peeled and chopped

## For the fajita seasoning

1 teaspoon mild chilli powder

¾ teaspoon ground cumin

¾ teaspoon sweet smoked paprika

¾ teaspoon unrefined sugar

½ teaspoon sea salt

¼ teaspoon onion powder

½ teaspoon garlic powder

pinch of cayenne pepper

A crowd-pleasing recipe – perfect for a family dinner – which brings together tender chicken, colourful peppers, avocado, black beans and brown rice, seasoned with a homemade fajita spice blend.

This goes brilliantly with the Black Bean & Corn Salad (see page 142).

Preheat the oven to 200°C, 180°C fan (400°F), Gas Mark 6.

To make the fajita seasoning, simply mix all the seasoning ingredients together.

On a baking sheet or baking tray, toss the peppers, onion and chicken in the fajita seasoning and olive oil. Bake in the oven for 25 minutes, or until the vegetables are soft and the chicken is cooked through. Stir in the beans, turn off the oven and leave the tray in there, to allow the beans to warm though.

Heat the brown rice, then stir through the lime juice and coriander. Divide the rice between 4 warmed bowls, topping it with the chicken and vegetables and the chopped avocado. Scatter with more coriander and serve with lime wedges.

Per portion:

| 430kcal | 20.4g fat | 3.8g sat fat | 20.1g protein | 8.2g fibre | 1.1g salt |

# SALMON WITH EGG-FRIED BROWN RICE, SPINACH & PEAS

**Mental Clarity**
**Anti-inflammatory**
**For Muscle**

## SERVES 2

2 skin-on salmon fillets

½ teaspoon clear honey

3 teaspoon soy sauce, plus more to serve

2.5cm (1-inch) piece of fresh root ginger, finely chopped, plus 5cm (2-inch) more, finely chopped

1 teaspoon extra virgin olive oil

1 onion, finely chopped

2 garlic cloves, finely chopped

50g (1¾oz) frozen peas

100g (3½oz) frozen spinach

200g (7oz) cooked brown rice

2 eggs

**Baked salmon, flaky and tender, is here served over egg-fried brown rice with spinach and sweet peas for added flavour. Great taste often comes from a balance of salt, sweet and fat, and that's exactly what this dish delivers.**

Preheat the oven to 200°C, 180°C fan (400°F), Gas Mark 6.

Place both salmon fillets on a small baking tray lined with baking paper and drizzle over the honey, then 1 teaspoon of the soy sauce. Scatter over the chopped 2.5cm (1-inch) piece of ginger. Place the tray in the oven for around 15 minutes, or until your salmon is cooked through.

Meanwhile, heat the oil in a frying pan and sauté the onion, the 5cm (2-inch) piece of fresh root ginger and the garlic for about 5 minutes, then add the peas and spinach. Break up the spinach with a spatula (this may take some time if using the blocks of frozen spinach, so be patient).

Add the rice and the remaining 2 teaspoons of soy sauce. Stir well to reheat the rice evenly.

Once the salmon is cooked, remove from the oven and stir the 2 eggs into the rice. You can break them straight in, then stir with the spatula to ensure even distribution.

Once the egg is cooked (this will take a matter of minutes) serve in warmed bowls with the salmon fillets on top, drizzled with soy sauce.

Per portion:

| 480kcal | 21g fat | 5.5g sat fat | 30g protein | 5g fibre | 2.3g salt |

# BAKED COD WITH TOMATO-BEAN RAGÙ

Blood Sugar
Anti-inflammatory
For Muscle

## SERVES 2

2 cod fillets, about 120g (4¼oz) each

1 teaspoon olive oil, plus more to cook the cod and serve

1 garlic clove, crushed

½ teaspoon smoked paprika, hot or sweet, as you prefer

Pinch of chilli flakes

400g (14oz) can of chopped tomatoes

400g (14oz) can of cannellini beans, drained and rinsed

¾ teaspoon balsamic vinegar

100g (3½oz) pitted black olives in oil, halved

Salt and pepper

Handful of parsley or basil leaves, to serve

Super-easy to prepare, this is a great way to get protein-rich fish into your diet on a busy weeknight evening. It is Mediterranean-inspired, with olives, garlic and herbs giving their distinctive flavours.

This makes a lovely meal with my Easy Tabbouleh (see page 139), to absorb the flavourful ragù.

Preheat the oven to 200°C, 180°C fan (400°F), Gas Mark 6.

Pat the cod dry and season both sides with salt, pepper and a drizzle of olive oil. Place on a baking tray lined with baking paper. Bake for 12 minutes, or until the fish flakes easily with a fork.

While the cod cooks, heat the 1 teaspoon of olive oil in a saucepan over a medium heat. Add the garlic, paprika and chilli flakes and cook for 30 seconds until fragrant.

Stir in the tomatoes, beans, balsamic vinegar and olives and season with salt and pepper. Reduce the heat to low and simmer gently for 8 minutes until slightly thickened and rich. Taste and adjust the seasoning, if needed.

Spoon the warm tomato-bean ragù into warmed shallow bowls. Place the baked cod on top, drizzle with a little olive oil, scatter with herbs, then serve.

Per portion:

| 300kcal | 10g fat | 1.2g sat fat | 30g protein | 10g fibre | 1.7g salt |

# TUNA & WHOLEGRAIN PASTA BAKE

Blood Sugar

For Muscle

**SERVES 4**

250g (9oz) wholegrain fusilli or
   penne pasta

1 tablespoon olive oil

1 leek, or 1 onion, finely chopped

2 garlic cloves, finely chopped

150g (5½oz) frozen peas

150g (5½oz) frozen sweetcorn

50g (1¾oz) butter, or olive oil

50g (1¾oz) wholemeal flour

550ml (1 pint) semi-skimmed milk

½–1 teaspoon Dijon mustard,
   to taste

120g (4¼oz) Cheddar or Red
   Leicester cheese, grated

1 teaspoon salt

½ teaspoon pepper

2 x 160g (5¾oz) cans of tuna in
   spring water or olive oil, drained

**A comforting, family-friendly dish of wholegrain pasta, canned tuna and vegetables in a creamy, cheesy sauce. It's designed to be both nutritious and satisfying, making it perfect for a busy weeknight.**

**This is great with a crunchy side of Cabbage & Carrot Slaw with Pumpkin Seeds (see page 136).**

Preheat the oven to 220°C, 200°C fan (425°F), Gas Mark 7.

Bring a large pot of salted water to the boil and cook the pasta until al dente (usually 1–2 minutes less than it says on the packet). Drain and set aside.

In a frying pan, heat the olive oil and sauté the leek or onion with the garlic until softened, but not coloured. Then add the frozen peas and sweetcorn and cook for about 5 minutes or until defrosted.

In a separate saucepan, melt the butter and stir in the flour to form a roux. Gradually whisk in the milk until smooth and thickened. Stir in the mustard, cheese, salt and pepper.

In a large mixing bowl, mix the drained pasta, tuna, sautéed veg and sauce. Transfer to a baking dish large enough to hold it all.

Bake in the oven for 15–20 minutes until golden and bubbling, then serve.

Per portion:

| 550kcal | 28g fat | 14.5g sat fat | 25g protein | 5.5g fibre | 4.2g salt |

# CHICKPEA & SPINACH CURRY

Heart Heathy

Blood Sugar

Vegan

### SERVES 4

1 tablespoon extra virgin olive oil

2 onions, finely chopped

2 garlic cloves, finely chopped

2.5cm (1-inch) piece of fresh root ginger, peeled and finely chopped

110g (4oz) frozen spinach

1 teaspoon sea salt

1 tablespoon mild curry powder

250ml (9fl oz) vegetable stock, made with ½ stock cube

400g (14oz) can of chickpeas, drained and rinsed

190g (6½oz) raw brown rice

400g (14oz) can of full-fat coconut milk

Juice of ½ lemon

**Gently spiced, brightened with a squeeze of lemon juice and served with brown rice, this is the perfect, satisfying vegan family dinner. It's easy to make and full of flavour.**

**Try it with Roasted Carrot & Lentil Mix (see page 140).**

In a large saucepan, heat the olive oil, then add the onions, garlic and ginger and sauté for 5 minutes. Add the spinach and sauté for a further few minutes, breaking it up with a wooden spoon (this may take some time if using the blocks of frozen spinach, so be patient).

Add the salt, curry powder, stock and chickpeas. Bring to the boil, then reduce the heat to a simmer and cook for 15 minutes.

Meanwhile, cook the rice according to the packet instructions. This amount should yield 400–500g (14oz–1lb 2oz) of cooked rice.

Once the curry has reduced slightly, add the coconut milk. Keep this at a simmer for a further 15 minutes, stirring occasionally; the curry should thicken even more. Just before serving, squeeze over the lemon juice and stir it in. Serve with the rice.

Per portion:

525kcal     22g fat     18g sat fat     9g protein     7g fibre     2g salt

# KALE PESTO WITH WHOLEGRAIN PASTA

Heart Heathy

Mental Clarity

Vegetarian

**SERVES 4**

60g (2¼oz) pine nuts

60g (2¼oz) kale or cavolo nero, coarse stalks removed, leaves washed and patted dry

90ml (6 tablespoons) extra virgin olive oil

50g (1¾oz) Parmesan cheese, vegetarian if needed, finely grated

1 small garlic clove, minced

Pepper

400g (14oz) wholegrain pasta

This combination of leafy greens and wholegrains brings both flavour and fibre to the table. Unlike traditional pesto, in which basil is mostly used for its aromatic qualities, kale and cavolo nero are leafy greens rich in dietary fibre, vitamins such as A, C and K and minerals such as calcium and iron.

Dry roast the pine nuts in a frying pan for 3–4 minutes, shaking regularly. Tip them into a food processor. Add the kale or cavolo nero, oil, Parmesan and garlic and crack in a good twist of pepper. Blend all the ingredients together, then check the seasoning and adjust accordingly.

Meanwhile, cook the pasta according to the packet instructions.

Stir the pesto into the just-cooked pasta and serve immediately.

**NOTE**

Pesto pasta is a regular part of most families' weekly meals. To boost the fibre content of yours each time, follow these easy tips:

Serve with toasted pumpkin seeds over the top, adding 1g fibre per 1 tablespoon.

Serve with a side salad, adding a further 1–2g fibre per portion.

Finely chop 2 tablespoons of sun-dried tomatoes and add to each portion for a further 1.5g fibre per portion.

Per portion:

| 710kcal | 38g fat | 6.1g sat fat | 20g protein | 8g fibre | 1.5g salt |

# RED LENTIL & COCONUT CURRY

Blood Sugar

For Muscle

Vegan

## SERVES 2

1 teaspoon extra virgin olive oil

1 small onion, chopped

1 tablespoon finely chopped garlic

1 tablespoon finely chopped fresh root ginger

1 teaspoon ground cumin

1 teaspoon nigella seeds

½ teaspoon ground turmeric

1 teaspoon sea salt

¼ teaspoon pepper

1 tablespoon tomato purée

100g (3½oz) split red lentils

50g (1¾oz) frozen spinach

150ml (¼ pint) full-fat coconut milk

250–300ml (9fl oz–½ pint) water

200g (7oz) cooked brown rice, to serve

**A protein-rich red lentil dish with creamy coconut milk and a blend of aromatic spices. This simple recipe delivers a delicious curry in less than 30 minutes.**

**It's great with a side of Turmeric Roasted Cauliflower (see page 145).**

Heat the oil in a saucepan over a medium heat and sauté the onion, garlic and ginger for 3–5 minutes or until softened but not coloured.

Add the spices, salt, pepper and tomato purée, then stir.

Add the lentils, spinach, coconut milk and 250ml (9fl oz) of the measured water. Bring to the boil, then reduce the heat to a simmer.

Cook for about 20 minutes or until the lentils are soft, stirring a couple of times. If the curry thickens or reduces too quickly, add more of the measured water.

Taste and check the seasonings, then serve with the brown rice.

Per portion:

| 430kcal | 20g fat | 14g sat fat | 18g protein | 8g fibre | 3.1g salt |

# ONE-PAN OVEN BARLEY RISOTTO WITH MUSHROOMS

## SERVES 2

1 tablespoon olive oil, or butter

1 small onion, finely chopped

2 garlic cloves, crushed

300g (10½oz) mushrooms, sliced (chestnut, button, or mixed)

200g (7oz) pearl barley, rinsed

550ml (1 pint) hot vegetable stock, made from 1 stock cube

30g (1oz) Parmesan cheese, vegetarian if needed, finely grated

Salt and pepper

3 tablespoons chopped parsley leaves, to serve

A wholesome twist on a classic. Using pearl barley instead of rice, this dish is baked in the oven for a hands-off approach, resulting in a creamy, hearty meal packed with earthy mushrooms and finished with Parmesan and parsley.

**Try it with Roasted Winter Vegetable Medley (see page 141).**

Preheat the oven to 200°C, 180°C fan (400°F), Gas Mark 6.

In an ovenproof pan with a lid, or a casserole dish, heat the oil or butter over a medium heat. Add the onion and cook for about 5 minutes or until soft but not coloured. Add the garlic and mushrooms and cook for 5–7 minutes, or until the mushrooms have given up their liquid and most of it has evaporated.

Stir in the barley to coat, then pour in the hot stock. Stir well.

Cover with a lid and bake in the oven for 35 minutes, or until the barley is tender and most of the liquid has been absorbed.

Stir in the Parmesan and adjust the seasoning. Scatter with the parsley, then serve.

Per portion:

| 522kcal | 12.5g fat | 3.9g sat fat | 11.1g protein | 18.7g fibre | 2.1g salt |

# BLACK BEAN TACOS

## SERVES 2

1 tablespoon olive oil

1 small red onion, finely chopped

2 garlic cloves, finely chopped

1 teaspoon ground cumin

½ teaspoon smoked paprika, hot or sweet, as you prefer

½ teaspoon ground coriander

400g (14oz) can of black beans, drained and rinsed

1 small yellow pepper, finely chopped

1 small courgette, finely chopped

Juice of ½ lime

Salt and pepper

## To serve

8 small wholemeal or corn tortillas

20g (¾oz) shredded lettuce

2 tomatoes, chopped

½ avocado, pitted, peeled and sliced

60g (2¼oz) Red Leicester cheese, vegetarian if needed, grated

20g (¾oz) coriander, chopped

**A hearty black bean filling made with vegetables and a sprinkle of cheese, all wrapped in wholesome corn or wheat tortillas. To switch it up, try the black bean mix as a nacho topping, with the same accompaniments. You will need about 120g (4¼oz) tortilla chips per person.**

Heat the olive oil in a saucepan over a medium heat. Sauté the onion for 3–4 minutes until soft but not coloured. Add the garlic and spices and cook for 1 minute until fragrant.

Stir in the black beans, yellow pepper and courgette. Cook for 5–7 minutes until the vegetables are tender, but not overcooked. If the beans are starchy, they may stick, so add a dash of water if this happens.

Mash just some of the beans lightly with a fork for texture. Add the lime juice and season to taste.

Meanwhile, warm the tortillas in a dry frying pan, microwave or oven.

Assemble the tacos: layer the bean filling, lettuce, tomatoes, avocado, cheese and coriander in the warmed tortillas.

Per portion:

| 650kcal | 27g fat | 8g sat fat | 23g protein | 20g fibre | 2.1g salt |

# WHITE BEAN & FETA ALL-IN-ONE BAKE

## SERVES 2

100g (3½oz) cherry tomatoes, halved

1 yellow or orange pepper, cut into cubes

1 red onion, sliced into wedges

1 tablespoon olive oil

½ teaspoon smoked paprika, hot or sweet, as you prefer

½ teaspoon dried oregano

Finely grated zest and juice of ½ lemon

400g (14oz) can of cherry tomatoes

400g (14oz) can of white beans, such as cannellini or butter beans, drained and rinsed

125g (4½oz) feta cheese, vegetarian if needed, cubed

2 tablespoons chopped parsley leaves

Salt and pepper

**Colourful vegetables, smooth white beans and tangy feta, this Mediterranean-inspired bake is roasted to bring out all the natural sweetness of the vegetables and enhance the creaminess of the feta.**

Preheat the oven to 200°C, 180°C fan (400°F), Gas Mark 6.

In a large baking tray or an ovenproof dish, mix the cherry tomatoes, yellow or orange pepper, onion, olive oil, paprika, oregano, lemon zest, salt and pepper. Bake for 25–30 minutes until the vegetables are soft and slightly caramelized.

Stir in the cans of cherry tomatoes and white beans, then scatter the feta cubes over the tray and return to oven for 10 minutes until the cheese is golden.

Finish with the lemon juice and parsley.

Per portion:

| 443kcal | 21g fat | 8g sat fat | 18g protein | 10g fibre | 2.5g salt |

# PUY LENTIL BURGERS

Weight Loss

Blood Sugar

Vegetarian/Vegan

## SERVES 3

1 teaspoon extra virgin olive oil
½ onion, finely chopped
1 carrot, finely chopped
1 celery stick, finely chopped
250g (9oz) cooked Puy lentils, or green lentils
200g (7oz) cooked peeled sweet potato
60g (2¼oz) cooked mushrooms, finely chopped
¾ teaspoon dried basil
¾ teaspoon sea salt
½ teaspoon balsamic vinegar

### To serve

3 wholegrain baps, or High Fibre Bread Rolls (see page 162)
30g (1oz) rocket
2 tablespoons mayonnaise, vegan if needed
2 tomatoes, sliced

Earthy Puy lentils, sweet potato and mushrooms create a satisfying veggie burger here. If you're looking for a healthy, protein-rich alternative to traditional burgers, this is it!

These go well with either or both of the Black Bean & Corn Salad and the Cabbage & Carrot Slaw with Pumpkin Seeds (see pages 142 and 136).

This recipe involves freezing the burgers overnight before cooking, so that they hold their shape, so do allow time for this in your meal planning.

Heat the oil in a wide, heavy-based pan. Add the onion, carrot and celery and fry for about 5 minutes until softened, but not coloured. Add the lentils and sweet potato and mash these down with a potato masher. Add the mushrooms, basil, salt and balsamic vinegar and turn off the heat. Leave to cool. Once fully cooled, mould into 6 burger shapes.

Place these on baking paper on a board in your freezer and allow to freeze overnight, or for up to 3 months.

The next day, preheat your oven to 220°C, 200°C fan (425°F), Gas Mark 7. Put the burgers on a baking sheet lined with baking paper and cook for 35 minutes, turning them over when there are 10 minutes to go.

Serve 2 burgers each in the baps or rolls with the rocket, mayo and tomatoes.

Per portion (2 burgers):

| 390kcal | 11g fat | 1.2g sat fat | 15g protein | 13g fibre | 2.2g salt |

# SIDES

# ROASTED BRUSSEL SPROUTS WITH LEMON TAHINI DRIZZLE

Blood Sugar
Anti-inflammatory
Vegan

**SERVES 4**

250g (9oz) Brussels sprouts
1 tablespoon extra virgin olive oil
Salt and pepper

### For the drizzle

2 tablespoons tahini
2 tablespoons extra virgin
 olive oil
1 tablespoon lemon juice
1 teaspoon chopped parsley
 leaves

**Roasting brings out the natural sweetness of Brussels sprouts, while the creamy lemon tahini sauce here adds a bright, nutty finish. This recipe is simple to prepare, making it perfect for weeknight winter dinners, and gives a whole new lease of life to Brussels sprouts.**

Preheat the oven to 200°C, 180°C fan (400°F), Gas Mark 6. Line a large baking sheet with baking paper.

Halve the Brussels sprouts lengthways and tip them into a mixing bowl. Add the olive oil, season with salt and pepper and toss to coat.

Tip the sprouts on to the prepared baking sheet and space them out as much as possible. Roast for 25 minutes, tossing once halfway.

While the sprouts are roasting, put all the tahini sauce ingredients into a small jar with a lid and season well. Seal the lid and shake well to combine.

Place the roasted sprouts on a serving dish and lightly drizzle with the tahini sauce to serve.

Per portion:

| 162kcal | 14.5g fat | 2g sat fat | 2.5g protein | 3g fibre | 0.7g salt |

# CABBAGE & CARROT SLAW WITH PUMPKIN SEEDS

Heart Heathy

Blood Sugar

Vegetarian/Vegan

## SERVES 4

125g (4½oz) red cabbage

125g (4½oz) green cabbage

125g (4½oz) carrots

2 tablespoons chopped parsley leaves

2 tablespoons pumpkin seeds

45g (1¾oz) sultanas, or raisins

### For the dressing

3 tablespoons extra virgin olive oil

2 tablespoons apple cider vinegar

1 tablespoon clear honey, or maple syrup

½ teaspoon Dijon mustard

Sea salt

**Bright, crunchy and colourful, this makes a refreshing side dish. It is quick to prepare, especially if you use a food processor for the veggies, and perfect to make ahead as the flavours deepen after a short marinating time in the refrigerator.**

There is a fast and a slow way to go about making this slaw. You can finely slice both colours of cabbage and coarsely grate the carrots (or julienne the carrots, if you have a julienne peeler). Or you can blitz all 3 in a food processor on a medium-low speed to chop them finely, which doesn't look as pretty, but is far quicker!

In a serving bowl, combine the prepared red and green cabbages, carrots and parsley.

Measure out the pumpkin seeds into a small frying pan. Dry-fry over a medium heat, stirring frequently, until the seeds are fragrant and starting to make little popping noises. Pour the toasted seeds into the serving bowl and toss to combine. Add the sultanas or raisins, too.

Make the dressing by putting all the ingredients in a small jar with a lid, adding a good pinch of salt. Seal and shake until thoroughly blended.

Drizzle the dressing over the slaw and toss until all the ingredients are lightly coated in dressing. Serve immediately, or cover and refrigerate to allow the slaw to marinate for up to several hours. If you leave it to marinate, be sure to bring it to room temperature and toss it again before serving.

Per portion:

| 110kcal | 6.2g fat | 0.5g sat fat | 3.5g protein | 3.5g fibre | 0.22g salt |

# EASY TABBOULEH

Heart Heathy

Weight Loss

Vegan

## SERVES 6

430ml (¾ pint) vegetable stock, made from 1 stock cube

215g (7½oz) medium bulgur wheat

3 spring onions, finely sliced

4 tomatoes, deseeded and finely chopped

Finely grated zest of 2 lemons, plus juice of 1 lemon

80g (2¾oz) parsley leaves, finely chopped

20g (¾oz) mint leaves, finely chopped

4 tablespoons olive oil

1 garlic clove, finely chopped

Salt and pepper

This simple Middle Eastern salad is made from a base of bulgur wheat, with crisp spring onions, juicy tomatoes, parsley, mint and a lemon dressing. The result is a light yet satisfying side dish that's perfect to take on picnics, or for a barbecue side, or as a healthy accompaniment to a main meal.

Pour the vegetable stock into a saucepan, set over a medium heat and bring to a gentle boil.

Stir in the bulgur wheat, then reduce the heat to low so the liquid simmers only very gently. Cover with a lid and cook for 12–15 minutes, stirring occasionally. The grains will absorb most of the liquid and soften.

Once the liquid is absorbed, remove the saucepan from the hob. Keep covered and let it stand for 5 minutes to allow the bulgur to finish steaming and separate, then remove the lid and use a fork to fluff through the grains. Taste and adjust with salt and pepper if needed, then leave to cool completely.

Simply stir all the other ingredients into the fluffy bulgur wheat, taste and adjust the seasoning if needed, then cover and store in the refrigerator for up to 3 days, until you're ready to serve.

Per portion:

| 225kcal | 9.9g fat | 1.1g sat fat | 4.5g protein | 5.4g fibre | 0.6g salt |

# ROASTED CARROT & LENTIL MIX

**Weight Loss**

**Anti-inflammatory**

Vegan

## SERVES 4

325g (11 ½oz) carrots, scrubbed and cut into 2cm (¾-inch) cubes

¾ teaspoon ground cumin

¼ teaspoon mild chilli powder

½ teaspoon garlic powder

1 teaspoon olive oil

2 tablespoons pine nuts

250g (9oz) cooked Puy lentils

3 tablespoons chopped parsley leaves

### For the dressing

2 tablespoons extra virgin olive oil

½ teaspoon Dijon mustard, or to taste

½ tablespoon maple syrup

1 tablespoon apple cider vinegar, or to taste

Salt and pepper

**This delicious, hearty dish is enlivened with cumin, chilli powder and garlic, finished with a tangy dressing and topped with toasted pine nuts for added crunch.**

Preheat the oven to 200°C, 180°C fan (400°F), Gas Mark 6.

Tip the carrot cubes into a baking tray and sprinkle over the spices and olive oil. Mix and roast for about 25 minutes, or until tender.

To make the dressing, combine all the ingredients in a jar with a lid, seasoning well with salt and pepper, then seal and shake to mix thoroughly. Taste and add salt, mustard or vinegar to taste.

Dry roast the pine nuts in a hot frying pan, stirring until they are fragrant. This will take a matter of minutes. Tip out on to a plate.

In a bowl, combine the cooked lentils and carrots. If you like, you can refrigerate these before serving for up to 24 hours, but bring to room temperature first.

Add the parsley and toasted pine nuts, then pour over the dressing, stir well and serve.

Per portion:

200kcal | 10.5g fat | 1.2g sat fat | 7g protein | 6g fibre | 0.8g salt

# ROASTED WINTER VEGETABLE MEDLEY

Heart Heathy

Anti-inflammatory

Vegan

**SERVES 4**

250g (9oz) sweet potatoes, scrubbed and cut into 3cm (1¼-inch) cubes

170g (6oz) Brussels sprouts, outer leaves removed, halved if very large

1 large red onion, sliced into 2cm (¾-inch) wide wedges

1 tablespoon extra virgin olive oil

1½ teaspoons thyme leaves

Salt and pepper

A wholesome dish in which the oven does all the work, bringing together sweet potatoes, Brussels sprouts and red onion, roasted to perfection, with thyme adding an aromatic finish. A delicious and comforting side for chilly days.

Preheat the oven to 220°C, 200°C fan (425°F), Gas Mark 7.

In a baking dish with sides, lay the veg out in a single layer. Add the olive oil, thyme and seasoning and toss to coat evenly.

Roast for 35 minutes, stirring once halfway, then serve.

Per portion:

126kcal     3.5g fat     0.5g sat fat     2g protein     4g fibre     0.7g salt

# BLACK BEAN & CORN SALAD

Weight Loss

Blood Sugar

Vegan

**SERVES 4**

400g (14oz) can of black beans, drained and rinsed

200g (7oz) can of sweetcorn, drained

1 tomato, finely chopped

1 ripe avocado, pitted, peeled and chopped

½ small red onion, finely chopped

20g (¾oz) coriander, finely chopped

1 small green chilli, deseeded and finely chopped

1 small garlic clove, minced

2 tablespoons lime juice, or to taste

1 tablespoon extra virgin olive oil

½ teaspoon ground cumin

Salt and pepper

A fresh, vibrant and boldly coloured no-cook Mexican-inflected side. Creamy avocado, coriander and green chilli enliven this nutrient-rich recipe, which is brought together with a zingy lime-based dressing.

In a serving bowl, combine all the ingredients and stir well.

Check the seasoning and add a little more lime juice, salt and pepper as required. Serve immediately.

Per portion:

245kcal    11.5g fat    1.2g sat fat    7g protein    8g fibre    0.27g salt

# TURMERIC ROASTED CAULIFLOWER

## SERVES 4

600g (1lb 5oz) cauliflower florets
1½ tablespoons olive oil
1½ teaspoons nigella seeds
¾ teaspoon ground turmeric
¼ teaspoon sea salt

**Bringing together turmeric and nigella seeds with the sweetness of roasted cauliflower florets, this makes an exceptional, super-easy side to curries. It's also amazingly flavoursome cold, as part of a spread of salads.**

Preheat the oven to 220°C, 200°C fan (425°F), Gas Mark 7.

Toss the cauliflower into a baking dish in which the florets can lie in a single layer. Add the oil, seeds, turmeric and salt and toss again to coat.

Roast for 35 minutes, turning halfway. The cauliflower is ready when it is slightly caramelized on the outside and offers little resistance when poked with a fork.

Serve hot or cold.

Per portion:

| 82kcal | 5.4g fat | 0.8g sat fat | 2.5g protein | 3.5g fibre | 0.4g salt |

# SNACKS

# BERRY & BEETROOT SMOOTHIE

**SERVES 2**

100g (3½oz) frozen raspberries

100g (3½oz) frozen blueberries

½ ripe banana

½ ripe avocado, pitted and peeled

100g (3½oz) cooked beetroot

250ml (9fl oz) semi-skimmed milk, or milk of your choice

1 teaspoon maple syrup (optional)

**A blend of frozen and fresh fruit with creamy avocado, your choice of milk and a touch of maple syrup. This is deliciously smooth, cheerfully bright-coloured and naturally sweet, as well as packed with antioxidants, vitamins and minerals.**

In a food processor or blender, combine all the ingredients and blitz until smooth.

Pour into glasses and drink straight away.

Per portion:

| 250kcal | 10g fat | 3.5g sat fat | 6g protein | 10g fibre | 0.18g salt |

# PEAR & CHIA SMOOTHIE

Heart Heathy

Anti-inflammatory

Vegetarian/Vegan

## SERVES 2

2 ripe pears, cored and chopped (total prepared weight about 250g / 9oz)

50g (1¾oz) spinach leaves

2 tablespoons chia seeds

250ml (9fl oz) almond milk, or milk of your choice, plus more if needed

½–1 tablespoon clear honey, or maple syrup

2 ice cubes

**Sweet, ripe pears and spinach, blended with creamy almond milk, this is a quick and easy way to boost your fibre intake and support digestion in liquid form.**

In a blender, combine all the ingredients. If you don't have a powerful blender, leave out the ice cubes and simply serve the smoothie over the top of an ice cube to cool it down. Blend until smooth and creamy. Leave for 5–10 minutes to settle and allow the chia seeds to soak up some of the milk.

If the smoothie is too thick, add more milk until you reach your desired consistency.

Pour into 2 glasses, over ice if you left it out while blending, and enjoy immediately.

Per portion:

| 330kcal | 10.5g fat | 0.3g sat fat | 4g protein | 10g fibre | 0.1g salt |

# APPLE & CINNAMON SMOOTHIE

**SERVES 1**

190g (6½oz) apple compote (see page 62)

100g (3½oz) 5 per cent fat Greek yogurt

90ml (6 tablespoons) semi-skimmed milk

Pinch of ground cinnamon

2 teaspoons milled (ground) flaxseed

½ teaspoon clear honey

2 ice cubes (optional)

**With the added benefits of milled (ground) flaxseed and a little honey, this smoothie is both satisfying and naturally sweet. Cinnamon adds its comfort to the glass.**

Put all the ingredients, except the ice cubes, in a blender and blend until smooth.

Add the ice cubes and blend again, if you want it extra-cold.

Pour into a glass and drink straight away.

Per portion:

| 230kcal | 8g fat | 3.9g sat fat | 13g protein | 4.5g fibre | 0.25g salt |

# GREEN GODDESS SMOOTHIE

Heart Heathy

Anti-inflammatory

Vegetarian/Vegan

## SERVES 1

1 ripe banana

30g (1oz) frozen spinach

85g (3oz) ripe avocado, pitted and peeled

200ml (7fl oz) semi-skimmed milk, or plant-based milk

90ml (6 tablespoons) apple juice

½ teaspoon honey, or maple syrup

**This deliciously green smoothie is an ideal way to fuel your morning, or recharge after a workout.**

Blend all the ingredients well in a food processor or blender.

Drink immediately.

Per portion (with semi-skimmed milk):

| 300kcal | 12g fat | 4g sat fat | 7g protein | 7g fibre | 0.25g salt |

# CUCUMBER & APPLE REFRESHER

Heart Heathy

Anti-inflammatory

Vegetarian/Vegan

## SERVES 2

1 large cucumber, peeled and chopped
2 apples, cored and chopped
Juice of 1 lemon
1–2 teaspoons maple syrup, or clear honey (optional)
A few mint leaves (optional)
250ml (9fl oz) coconut water
Ice cubes

**Such a hydrating drink, this combines fruit and vegetables with lemon juice and coconut water. It is ideal when you want to cool off on a warm day, or simply need a pick-me-up any time.**

Place the cucumber, apples, lemon juice, 1 teaspoon of the maple syrup or honey and mint leaves, if using, into a blender. Add the coconut water and blend until completely smooth.

Taste and adjust the sweetness, if needed, with the remaining maple syrup or honey.

Chill in the refrigerator for at least 30 minutes, or serve immediately over ice.

Per portion:

| 160kcal | 0.55g fat | 0.05g sat fat | 1.25g protein | 5g fibre | 0.1g salt |

# AVO-BERRY THICKSHAKE

Heart Healthy

Mental Clarity

Vegetarian

SERVES 2

40g (1½oz) oat flour (if you can't find this, blend regular oats in a food processor)

100g (3½oz) frozen blueberries

190g (6½oz) natural yogurt

150g (5½oz) frozen ripe avocado

300ml (½ pint) almond milk

**Frozen blueberries bring vibrant colour and antioxidants, while ripe avocado adds a luxurious creaminess and heart healthy fats. Oat flour and natural yogurt help this thickshake to deliver slow release energy, fibre and a gentle protein boost.**

Blitz all the ingredients in a blender or food processor, then serve immediately.

Per portion:

305kcal

16g fat

3.4g sat fat

9g protein

7g fibre

0.3g salt

# FLAXSEED CRACKERS

Heart Heathy

Weight Loss

Vegan

MAKES 16

65g (2½oz) milled (ground)
   flaxseed
15g (½oz) chia seeds
¼ teaspoon salt
½ teaspoon mixed herbs
125ml (4fl oz) water

**A wholesome, crunchy snack, naturally gluten free, high in fibre and easy to prepare. These crackers are ideal to serve with your favourite dips.**

Combine the ground flaxseed, chia seeds, salt and herbs in a mixing bowl. Stir in the measured water: the mixture will thicken into a gel-like dough. Let the dough sit for 10 minutes to firm up.

Preheat the oven to 190°C, 170°C fan (375°F), Gas Mark 5.

Spread the cracker mixture thinly and evenly on to a baking tray lined with baking paper, aiming for it to lie 2–3mm (⅛ inch) deep. It's important that the mixture is spread evenly, for even cooking and crisping.

Score into 16 squares with a knife, for easy breaking later.

Bake for 35 minutes.

Remove and allow to cool a little, then break the crackers apart along the scored lines and turn each of them over. Pop back into the oven for a further 5–10 minutes to crisp up their undersides. If some are thicker, just cook them for a little longer until all are crisp and golden. Cool completely, then serve. These will keep in an airtight container for 2 days.

Per portion (per cracker):

| 26kcal | 2g fat | 0.04g sat fat | 1g protein | 1.5g fibre | 0.1g salt |

# ROASTED PEAS WITH SMOKED PAPRIKA

Heart Heathy

For Muscle

Vegan

## SERVES 2 AS A SNACK

240g (8½oz) frozen peas, left at room temperature to defrost for up to 4 hours

½ teaspoon salt

1 teaspoon smoked paprika, hot or sweet, as you prefer

2 teaspoons extra virgin olive oil

**A straightforward way to transform frozen peas into a crispy, savoury treat. With just 4 store cupboard ingredients, this recipe provides a simple, nutritious alternative that can help overcome that craving for crisps.**

Preheat the oven to 200°C, 180°C fan (400°F), Gas Mark 6. Line a baking sheet with baking paper.

Pat the peas dry with kitchen paper, then toss in a bowl with the salt, paprika and oil. Lay them on the prepared baking sheet so the peas are in a single layer.

Bake for 35–40 minutes until the pears are starting to get a good colour. They crisp up further as they cool, so they don't need to be super-crispy when you remove them from the oven, just well coloured.

Eat within 24 hours.

Per portion:

| 135kcal | 5.7g fat | 0.6g sat fat | 6g protein | 6g fibre | 1.4g salt |

# APRICOT & OAT BRUNCH BARS

Heart Heathy

Anti-inflammatory

Vegan

**SERVES 6**

A little flavourless oil, for the tin

30g (1oz) shelled hemp seeds

120g (4¼oz) rolled oats

70g (2½oz) maple syrup

120g (4¼oz) almond butter

4 ripe bananas, peeled and mashed

70g (2½oz) dried apricots, chopped

**Bananas and dried apricots with the hearty texture of oats and hemp seeds, these bars are great for a post-workout snack or on-the-go breakfast or brunch.**

Preheat the oven to 210°C, 190°C fan (410°F), Gas Mark 6½. Oil a 900g (2lb) loaf tin and line it with baking paper.

Mix all the ingredients together in a mixing bowl, then pour into the prepared tin and press down evenly with the back of a spoon.

Pop into the preheated oven and cook for 40 minutes.

Leave until cool enough to handle before removing from the tin, but don't let it get cold before you slice it into 6 bars. Leave to cool completely on a wire rack. These will keep in an airtight container in the refrigerator for up to 1 week.

Per portion:

| 353kcal | 14.3g fat | 2.1g sat fat | 10g protein | 7g fibre | 0.05g salt |

# OAT & ALMOND ENERGY BITES

Heart Heathy

For Muscle

Vegetarian/Vegan

## MAKES 6

60g (2¼oz) rolled oats

20g (¾oz) ground almonds

1 tablespoon chia seeds

1 tablespoon milled (ground) flaxseed

15g (½oz) dried cranberries, or raisins

40g (1½oz) almond butter

1½ tablespoons clear honey, or maple syrup

½ teaspoon vanilla extract

Salt

**The best thing about these tasty little spheres is that they are no-bake, so everyone can help to make them, even the youngest members of your household. Designed to deliver sustained energy and digestive benefits, they're perfect for on-the-go snacking, or post-exercise refuelling.**

Combine the oats, ground almonds, chia seeds, flaxseed, cranberries or raisins and a pinch of salt in a large mixing bowl.

Stir in the almond butter, honey or maple syrup and vanilla and mix until sticky and well combined.

Roll the mixture into 6 small balls, about 25g (1oz) each and place on a baking tray lined with baking paper. Refrigerate for at least 30 minutes, to firm up.

Store in an airtight container in the refrigerator for up to 1 week.

Per portion (per bite):

135kcal     7g fat     0.7g sat fat     4.5g protein     4g fibre     0.06g salt

# HIGH FIBRE BREAD ROLLS

## MAKES 4

300g (10½oz) cottage cheese
2 large eggs
200g (7oz) rolled oats
2 tablespoons milled (ground) flaxseed
50g (1¾oz) mixed seeds, such as pumpkin, sunflower, poppy or sesame
2 teaspoons baking powder
Salt

**Made using a blend of oats, protein-rich cottage cheese and a variety of seeds, these rolls are designed not only to boost your daily fibre intake, but also to keep you feeling fuller for longer.**

Preheat the oven to 200°C, 180°C fan (400°F), Gas Mark 6. Line a baking sheet with baking paper.

In a bowl, mix the cottage cheese and eggs.

In a separate bowl, mix the oats, flaxseed, mixed seeds, baking powder and a pinch of salt. Stir in the wet ingredients until just combined.

Split into 4 portions and mould each into a bap. Place on the prepared baking sheet and bake for 30 minutes until golden brown on the outside.

Cool thoroughly before splitting and eating.

These will keep in an airtight container in a cool part of the kitchen, or the refrigerator, for up to 3 days.

Per portion:

| 360kcal | 15g fat | 2.1g sat fat | 28g protein | 12g fibre | 0.64g salt |

# DESSERT

# OAT & NUT CRUMBLE WITH DARK BERRIES

Heart Heathy
Mental Clarity
Vegetarian

**SERVES 4**

300g (10½oz) frozen berries, ideally half each blackberries and blueberries

2 teaspoons clear honey, or maple syrup

1 teaspoon vanilla extract

90g (3¼oz) rolled oats

65g (2¼oz) wholemeal flour, or Wholegrain Gluten-free Flour (see page 46)

2 tablespoons chopped hazelnuts

1 tablespoon oat bran

20g (¾oz) unrefined sugar, I love coconut sugar

¼ teaspoon ground allspice

1 tablespoon chia seeds

65g (2¼oz) butter, melted

With just a few simple changes to a classic crumble, this recipe offers a higher fibre twist. Wholemeal flour, oat bran, nuts and chia seeds create a crumble topping that's delicious, nutritious and supports better digestion.

Preheat the oven to 210°C, 190°C fan (410°F), Gas Mark 6½.

Place the fruit into a 25 x 15cm or 20 x 20cm (10 x 6 inches or 8 x 8 inches) baking dish. Drizzle over the honey and vanilla extract.

In a separate bowl, mix the oats, flour, nuts, oat bran, sugar, spice and chia seeds, then stir in the melted butter until evenly distributed and cover the fruit with this crumble mix.

Pop into the oven to bake for 20–25 minutes or until golden brown on top. Serve hot or cold.

Per portion:

| 373kcal | 18g fat | 8.5g sat fat | 6.5g protein | 8g fibre | 0.05g salt |

# FUDGY FLOURLESS CHOCOLATE BROWNIES

**SERVES 8**

80g (2¾oz) salted butter, cubed, plus more for the dish

80g (2¾oz) almond butter

100g (3½oz) maple syrup

35g (1¼oz) cocoa powder, or cacao powder

135g (4¾oz) ground almonds

2 large eggs, lightly beaten

60g (2¼oz) dark chocolate chips

60g (2¼oz) chopped walnuts

Salt

**If you want the ultimate chocolate indulgence that's both rich in flavour and naturally gluten-free, these will become a favourite, combining the intense taste of cocoa or cacao with creamy almond butter and the satisfying crunch of walnuts. Whether you're catering for gluten-free diets or simply craving a decadent dessert, these are easy to make and perfect for sharing at gatherings, giving to friends, or enjoying as a treat with a cup of coffee or tea.**

Preheat the oven to 190°C, 170°C fan (375°F), Gas Mark 5. Butter a 25 x 15cm or 20 x 20cm (10 x 6 inch or 8 x 8 inch) rectangular or square baking dish and line it with baking paper.

In a small saucepan over a low heat, melt the butter, nut butter and maple syrup together with a pinch of salt until combined. Remove from the heat.

Add the cocoa or cacao and ground almonds, stir well and leave to cool.

Once cooled, add the eggs and stir to combine. Fold in the chocolate chips and walnuts.

Spoon the mixture into the prepared tin, smoothing down the top with the back of a spoon. Bake for 25 minutes, then place the dish on a wire rack to cool fully.

Slice into 8 squares or bars to serve. These will keep in an airtight container for up to 1 week.

Per portion:

| 370kcal | 30g fat | 8.4g sat fat | 9g protein | 3g fibre | 0.24g salt |

# FLAXSEED CHOCOLATE SLICES

Low FODMAP

Heart Heathy

Vegetarian/Vegan

## SERVES 8

45g (1½oz) cocoa powder, or cacao powder

45g (1½oz) milled (ground) flaxseed

1 teaspoon bicarbonate of soda

125ml (4fl oz) full-fat milk, or plant-based milk

1 egg

1 teaspoon vanilla extract

4 tablespoons maple syrup, or to taste

1 heaped tablespoon almond butter, or peanut butter

35g (1¼oz) dark chocolate chips

Salt

**Looking for a delicious alternative to a brownie, that's also better for you? If so, these chocolate slices – a wholesome twist on the classic – are for you. They use flaxseed as a base and are sweetened naturally with maple syrup instead of refined sugar.**

Preheat the oven to 190°C, 170°C fan (375°F), Gas Mark 5. Line a 900g (2lb) loaf tin with baking paper.

In a bowl, mix together the cocoa or cacao powder, flaxseed, bicarbonate of soda and a pinch of salt.

In a separate bowl, whisk the milk, egg, vanilla, maple syrup and nut butter.

Combine the wet and dry ingredients and stir, then gently fold in the chocolate chips.

Pour into the prepared loaf tin and bake for 20–25 minutes until a cocktail stick poked into the centre comes out clean.

Leave the tin to cool completely on a wire rack, then slice into 8 portions. These will keep in an airtight container for up to 3 days, or freeze for up to 3 months.

Per portion:

| 140kcal | 5.5g fat | 1.9g sat fat | 3.5g protein | 3g fibre | 0.1g salt |

# AVOCADO CHOCOLATE MOUSSE

Mental Clarity

Anti-inflammatory

Vegetarian/Vegan

## SERVES 4

2 ripe avocados (see recipe introduction), pitted and peeled

60g (2¼oz) dark chocolate chips, vegan if needed, melted

1 tablespoon cocoa powder, or cacao powder

50ml (2fl oz) semi-skimmed milk, or milk of your choice, plus more if needed

Dash of vanilla extract

2 tablespoons maple syrup

Pinch of sea salt

**As nourishing as it is decadent. By blending ripe avocados with rich cacao, dark chocolate, a touch of maple syrup and a hint of vanilla, you create a velvety-smooth treat. The avocados must be ripe for this, or they won't whip up into a mousse.**

**You will need a high-speed blender or food processor to make this recipe.**

Simply combine all the ingredients in a high-speed blender or food processor. Start by blending at high speed, then reduce the speed to low and continue to process until you have a velvety smooth mousse.

If your avocado is not blending well, add a dash more milk until you reach a smooth consistency. Keep blending until smooth; you will need to keep scraping down the sides of your blender. Have patience!

Pour into 4 small glass jars or ramekins and leave to set in the refrigerator overnight, then serve the next day.

Per portion:

| | | | or slightly less if using plant-based milk | | |
|---|---|---|---|---|---|
| 235kcal | 16.5g fat | 7g sat fat | 3.5g protein | 7g fibre | 0.07g salt |

# FRUIT & NUT CHOCOLATE BARS

Heart Heathy

Anti-inflammatory

Vegan

## MAKES 18

100g (3½oz) medjool dates
30g (1oz) walnuts
30g (1oz) pecans
100g (3½oz) peanut butter
30g (1oz) pumpkin seeds
30g (1oz) goji berries
50g (1¾oz) puffed quinoa
375g (13oz) plain dark
  chocolate, vegan if needed,
  melted

**A delicious, no-bake bar that combines the natural sweetness of medjool dates with the crunch of pumpkin seeds and puffed quinoa and the tart burst of goji berries.**

Find a baking sheet that measures 20 x 15cm (8 x 6 inches) and line it with baking paper.

In a food processor, blend the dates and nuts until you have a crumb-like texture.

Stir in the peanut butter, pumpkin seeds, goji berries and puffed quinoa.

Finally, stir in the melted chocolate and push the whole mixture into the prepared baking sheet with the back of a spoon, so it lies in an even layer. Leave to set.

Once set, slice into 18 bars. You can store these at room temperature in an airtight container for 1 week until you're ready to eat, though the puffed rice gets less crunchy.

Per portion:

| 200kcal | 12.5g fat | 8g sat fat | 3.5g protein | 3g fibre | 0.04g salt |

# GLUTEN-FREE FLAXSEED BANANA BREAD

Low FODMAP

Heart Heathy

Vegetarian

**SERVES 8**

4 ripe bananas

1 large egg, lightly beaten

65g (2¼oz) salted butter, softened

1 teaspoon vanilla extract

65g (2¼oz) unrefined sugar

190g (6½oz) Wholegrain Gluten-Free Flour (self-raising version, see page 46, or see note, below)

**A wholesome twist on classic banana bread. This recipe combines ripe bananas, flaxseed and a gluten-free flour blend to create a moist loaf. Whether you're following a gluten-free diet, looking for nourishing bakes, or just fancy a delicious banana bread, this hits the mark.**

Preheat the oven to 190°C, 170°C fan (375°F), Gas Mark 5. Line a 450g (1lb) loaf tin with baking paper.

In a large bowl, mash the bananas with a fork. Add the egg, butter and vanilla and stir well.

In a separate bowl, blend the dry ingredients (see note, below). Mix this into the wet ingredients and stir to combine.

Pour the batter into the prepared loaf tin and bake for 50 minutes, or until a cocktail stick inserted into the centre comes out clean. Remove, then leave to cool on a wire rack. Once cool, slice and serve. This will keep in the refrigerator for up to 1 week.

---

**NOTE**

It's easy to whip up a batch of my Wholegrain Gluten-free Flour (see page 46), so I recommend that you do, but you can create a single portion for this recipe as follows. (I don't recommend using store-bought blends, which often contain unwanted additives or ultra-processed ingredients.) Simply combine:

85g (3oz) buckwheat flour

50g (1¾oz) brown rice flour

25g (1oz) arrowroot powder

20g (¾oz) milled (ground) flaxseed

½ teaspoon baking powder

½ teaspoon bicarbonate of soda

---

Per portion:

237kcal    8.9g fat    4.3g sat fat    2.5g protein    3.25g fibre    0.26g salt

# APPLES, ALMOND BUTTER & HEMP

## SERVES 2

2 crisp eating apples
1 teaspoon lemon juice (optional)
4 tablespoons almond butter
2 teaspoons shelled hemp seeds
Good pinch of ground cinnamon

## Suggested toppings (optional)

Chia seeds
Dessicated coconut
Granola (see page 50 for
  homemade)
Dark chocolate chips, vegan
  if needed

**This combination provides a boost of fibre, protein and healthy fats. The recipe is easy to customize with extra toppings, making it a versatile choice that's easy to switch up every day, keeping things interesting.**

Rinse the apples thoroughly and pat dry. Slice into thin wedges or rounds, discarding the cores. Toss with lemon juice, if you like, to prevent them browning.

Arrange the apple slices on plates. Spread almond butter generously over each slice.

Sprinkle hemp seeds evenly over the almond butter-topped apple slices, then finish with a sprinkle of cinnamon and any of the other suggested toppings you fancy. Enjoy immediately.

Per portion (with all the toppings):

| 305kcal | 19.7g fat | 3.3g sat fat | 8.5g protein | 7g fibre | 0.1g salt |

# CHICKPEA CHOCOLATE CHIP COOKIES

Heart Heathy

Mental Clarity

Vegan

## SERVES 10

400g (14oz) can of chickpeas, drained but liquid reserved, rinsed

3 tablespoons melted coconut oil

1 tablespoon vanilla extract

60g (2¼oz) oat flour (see recipe introduction)

20g (¾oz) oat bran, plus more if needed

90g (3¼oz) unrefined sugar

½ teaspoon salt

½ teaspoon bicarbonate of soda

1 teaspoon apple cider vinegar

80g (2¾oz) dark chocolate chips, vegan if needed

**This recipe uses blitzed chickpeas as a base, making the cookies naturally high in fibre and protein. They also use plant-based fat, and can easily be made gluten-free by using gluten-free oats and oat bran. To make oat flour, simply grind rolled oats in a food processor until fine.**

Preheat the oven to 200°C, 180°C fan (400°F), Gas Mark 6 and line a baking tray with baking paper.

Process the chickpeas, coconut oil and vanilla in a food processor until relatively smooth.

In a separate bowl, combine the oat flour, oat bran, sugar, salt and bicarbonate of soda. Add this to the food processor with the apple cider vinegar. Process to bring everything together into a smooth batter. Fold in the chocolate chips until evenly distributed throughout the cookie dough.

If the dough seems a little wet, add a little more oat bran. If it seems a little dry, add some of the liquid drained from the chickpeas (this liquid is known as aquafaba).

Shape the dough into 10 equal cookies on the prepared baking sheet and press each down with the back of a spoon, or gently with your fingers.

Pop into the oven and cook for about 20 minutes until the edges are starting to crisp up and the tops look brown.

Remove from the oven and cool completely before serving. These will keep in an airtight container for up to 3 days.

Per portion (per cookie):

| 170kcal | 7.5g fat | 4g sat fat | 3g protein | 2.5g fibre | 0.35g salt |

# DATE & WALNUT CHOCOLATE BALLS

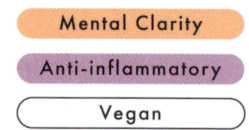

**Mental Clarity**

**Anti-inflammatory**

Vegan

**SERVES 8**

110g (4oz) walnut halves

190g (6½oz) medjool dates

2 tablespoons cocoa powder, or cacao powder

3 tablespoons desiccated coconut (optional)

Salt

**Made with just a handful of wholesome ingredients, these energy balls are chocolaty, naturally sweet, rich in healthy fats and make a satisfying snack or light dessert.**

Simply grind the nuts in a food processor, then add the dates, cocoa or cacao and a pinch of salt and blend again.

Blend for long enough that some of the natural fats are released from the walnuts, so the mixture can be formed into balls. This may take some patience and regular scraping down of the sides of the processor.

Roll into 8 balls – each 40–45g (1½–1¾oz) – between your palms. If you'd like even greater flavour and more fibre, then roll each ball in desiccated coconut.

Leave in the refrigerator to cool and store for up to 1 week.

Per portion (without coconut):

| 160kcal | 9g fat | 1g sat fat | 2.5g protein | 3g fibre | 0.05g salt |

# BERRY & AVOCADO ICE CREAM

Mental Clarity

Anti-inflammatory

Vegan

## SERVES 2

100g (3½oz) frozen raspberries
110g (4oz) frozen sliced banana
90g (3¼oz) pitted and peeled
very ripe avocado (see recipe
introduction)

A high-fibre, naturally sweet treat which is great for gut health, satiety and blood sugar balance. Raspberries and avocado are especially rich in insoluble fibre, while banana adds soluble fibre for digestive support.

As with the chocolate mousse recipe (see page 171), the avocado needs to be very ripe here, in order to whip up to the texture you want in an ice cream.

Simply blend all the ingredients together. (Depending on how powerful your food processor is, you may need to leave the fruit to defrost a little before blending.) Start at high speed, then scrape down the sides and reduce the speed to medium to combine all the ingredients to a smooth consistency.

Serve immediately, while the ice cream is still super-cold.

Per portion:

| 145kcal | 7.4g fat | 1.1g sat fat | 2g protein | 7g fibre | 0.02g salt |

# ENDNOTES

**1** Bakr, A. F., & Farag, M. A. (2023). Soluble dietary fibers as antihyperlipidemic agents: A comprehensive review to maximize their health benefits. *ACS Omega, 8*(28), 24680–24694. https://doi.org/10.1021/acsomega.3c01121

**2** Giuntini, E. B., Sardá, F. A. H., & de Menezes, E. W. (2022). The effects of soluble dietary fibers on glycemic response: An overview and future perspectives. *Foods, 11*(3934). https://doi.org/10.3390/foods11233934

**3** Costabile, A., Deaville, E. R., Morales, A. M., & Gibson, G. R. (2016). Prebiotic potential of a maize-based soluble fibre and impact of dose on the human gut microbiota. *PLoS ONE, 11*(1), e0144457. https://doi.org/10.1371/journal.pone.0144457

**4** Mahmood, W. M., Abraham Nordling, M., Håkansson, N., Wolk, A., & Hjern, F. (2021). High intake of dietary fibre from fruit and vegetables reduces the risk of hospitalisation for diverticular disease. *International Journal of Colorectal Disease, 36*(6), 1231–1238. https://pubmed.ncbi.nlm.nih.gov/30084005/

**5** Oh H, Kim H, Lee DH, *et al*. Different dietary fibre sources and risks of colorectal cancer and adenoma: a dose–response meta-analysis of prospective studies. *British Journal of Nutrition*. 2019;122(6):605-615. doi:10.1017/S0007114519001454 https://pubmed.ncbi.nlm.nih.gov/31495339/

**6** Inoue, R.; Suzuki, K.; Takaoka, M.; Narumi, M.; Naito, Y. Effects of Dietary Fiber Supplementation on Gut Microbiota and Bowel Function in Healthy Adults: A Randomized Controlled Trial. *Microorganisms* 2025, 13, 2068. https://doi.org/10.3390/microorganisms13092068

**7** Sanders, L. M., Dicklin, M. R., Palacios, O. M., Maki, C. E., Wilcox, M. L., & Maki, K. C. (2020). Effects of potato resistant starch intake on insulin sensitivity, related metabolic markers and appetite ratings in men and women at risk for type 2 diabetes: A pilot cross over randomised controlled trial. *Journal of Human Nutrition and Dietetics, 34*(1), 94–105. https://doi.org/10.1111/jhn.12822

**8** Freijy, T. M., Cribb, L., Oliver, G., Metri, N.-J., Opie, R. S., Jacka, F. N., Hawrelak, J. A., Rucklidge, J. J., Ng, C.H., & Sarris, J. (2023). Effects of a high-prebiotic diet versus probiotic supplements versus synbiotics on adult mental health: The "Gut Feelings" randomised controlled trial. *Frontiers in Neuroscience, 16*, 1097278. https://doi.org/10.3389/fnins.2022.1097278

**9** Inoue, R., Suzuki, K., Takaoka, M., Narumi, M., & Naito, Y. (2025). Effects of dietary fiber supplementation on gut microbiota and bowel function in healthy adults: A randomized controlled trial. *Microorganisms, 13*, 2068. https://doi.org/10.3390/microorganisms13092068

**10** Ultra-Processed Food as a % of Household Food Consumption. (n.d.). Brilliant Maps. Retrieved from https://publichealth.jhu.edu/2024/ultraprocessed-foods-account-for-more-than-half-of-calories-consumed-at-home

**11** Belete, T., & Yadete, E. (2023). Effect of mono cropping on soil health and fertility management for sustainable agriculture practices: A review. *Journal of Plant Sciences*, 11(6), 192–197. https://www.sciencepublishinggroup.com/article/10.11648/j.jps.20231106.13

**12** Marino, M., Puppo, F., Del Bo', C., Vinelli, V., Riso, P., Porrini, M., & Martini, D. (2021). A systematic review of worldwide consumption of ultra-processed foods: Findings and criticisms. *Nutrients*, 13(8), 2778. https://pubmed.ncbi.nlm.nih.gov/34444936/

# UK/US GLOSSARY

| | |
|---|---|
| Baking paper | Parchment paper |
| Beetroot | Beet |
| Bicarbonate of soda | Baking soda |
| Black beans | Turtle beans |
| Butter beans | Lima beans |
| Celeriac | Celery root |
| Chickpeas | Garbanzo beans |
| Coriander (fresh) | Cilantro |
| Courgette | Zucchini |
| Desiccated coconut | Dried shredded coconut |
| Flaked almonds | Slivered almonds |
| Flour, plain/self-raising | Flour, all-purpose/self-rising |
| Frying pan | Skillet |
| Grated | Shredded |
| Ground almonds | Almond meal |
| Jug | Pitcher |
| Kitchen paper | Paper towel |
| Loaf tin | Loaf pan |
| Minced beef | Ground beef |
| Natural yogurt | Plain yogurt |
| Pepper (red) | Bell pepper |
| Plain dark chocolate | Semi-sweet chocolate |
| Porridge | Oatmeal |
| Rocket | Arugula |
| Spring onion | Scallion |
| Stock | Broth |
| Sultanas | Golden raisins |
| Tomato purée | Tomato paste |

# INDEX

# ACKNOWLEDGEMENTS

No cookbook is ever created alone, and *The Ultimate High Fibre Handbook* is the result of the hard work and creative talent of many wonderful people.

First and foremost, my thanks must go to my incredible recipe testers. Your feedback helped shape these recipes into dishes that truly work in real kitchens. Thank you for taking the time to cook, taste, tweak and report back Kate Taylor, Jen Roach, Vicki Hazel, Gill Smart, Shona Lockie and Sam Coombs.

I am extremely grateful to Ruby Shorrock, who generously contributed to the nutritional information for these recipes.

This book came to life visually thanks to a very talented creative team. Thank you to Andrew Burton, whose photography captured both the colour and comfort of these dishes. I'm equally grateful to Emily Jonzen for making every plate look as delicious as it tastes. A special thank you to Juliette Norsworthy for bringing together the visual identity of the book with such care.

My sincere thanks go to Kate Fox whose encouragement and editorial input helped shape this book from early concept to finished product. I'm also very grateful to both Sybella Stephens and Vicky Orchard for your attention to detail and suggestions that helped strengthen each chapter.

Finally, my appreciation goes to Jane Graham Maw whose support and advocacy made this book possible.

To everyone who contributed your time and enthusiasm to *The Ultimate High Fibre Handbook* thank you for helping bring this book to life.

First published in Great Britain in 2026 by Hamlyn, an imprint of
Octopus Publishing Group Ltd
Carmelite House
50 Victoria Embankment
London EC4Y 0DZ
www.octopusbooks.co.uk

An Hachette UK Company
www.hachette.co.uk

The authorized representative in the EEA is Hachette Ireland,
8 Castlecourt Centre, Dublin 15, D15 XTP3, Ireland (email: info@hbgi.ie)

Distributed in the US by Hachette Book Group
1290 Avenue of the Americas, 4th and 5th Floors
New York, NY 10104

Distributed in Canada by Canadian Manda Group
664 Annette St., Toronto, Ontario, Canada M6S 2C8

ISBN: 978 0 60064 046 2
eISBN: 978 0 60064 047 9

A CIP catalogue record for this book is available from the British Library.

Printed and bound in Germany.

10 9 8 7 6 5 4 3 2 1

**Publisher:** Kate Fox
**Art Director:** Juliette Norsworthy
**Photographer:** Andrew Burton
**Food Stylist:** Emily Jonzen
**Props Stylist:** Max Robinson
**Production Controllers:** Lucy Carter & Nic Jones